ELIZABETH R. EPPERLY

Anthony Trollope's Notes on the Old Drama

English Literary Studies
University of Victoria
1988

ENGLISH LITERARY STUDIES
Published at the University of Victoria

ISBN 0-920604-37-4

The ELS Monograph Series is published in consultation with members of the Department by ENGLISH LITERARY STUDIES, Department of English, University of Victoria, B.C., Canada, V8W 2Y2.

ELS Monograph Series No. 42
© 1988 by Elizabeth R. Epperly

For
Elizabeth and Harold Larsen
Andrew, Mark, and Karen Houston-Walsh

CONTENTS

ACKNOWLEDGMENTS

I thank the Folger Shakespeare Library in Washington, D.C., for permission to publish Trollope's manuscript notes and the librarians of the Folger for their cheerful, helpful attention.

My thanks to *Notes & Queries* and *English Studies in Canada* for permission to republish articles that originally appeared in their pages. (These two pieces have been altered here to include Trollope material that escaped me earlier: Dyce's edition of Shakespeare, Hawkins' volume with Trollope's notes, and the marginal notations in Halliwell's *Dictionary of Old English Plays.*)

I would also like to thank the Social Sciences and Humanities Research Council of Canada for the time and funding that made parts of this study possible.

Throughout this study, I have used, when possible, abbreviations when referring to the edition of plays Trollope was reading.

In "Trollope Reading Old Drama" I have put into parentheses this information: (abbreviated form of editor's or playwright's name [depending on the edition Trollope was using], volume number in which the play commentary appears, page number of the play commentary).

Accompanying Trollope's comments, I have given, in parentheses: (the editor's name, volume number, page number); the title of the play; in square brackets: [the name of the playwright (where appropriate) and any other edition in which Trollope includes commentary on this same play]. As noted in my introduction, Trollope often copied verbatim his own comments from one play edition to another. When he has merely copied his own words, I say, in square brackets: [verbatim in (editor, volume, page)]. When Trollope makes only insignificant changes in punctuation or spelling, I say, in square brackets: [virtually identical in]. Other times Trollope copies the comment but makes changes in it *or* he writes a different comment altogether. These changed or different comments I indicate with the word "compare": [compare (editor, volume, page)]. Sometimes Trollope writes out his comment only once and simply refers to another edition for his original comment. In the square brackets following an original comment that is referred to elsewhere, I use the abbreviation "cr." (cross-referenced) to show that the edition referred to has only a reference and no additional commentary or copied commentary: [cr. (editor, volume, page)]. Following the cross-referenced entry, the square brackets will use the word "see" to indicate where the full commentary may be found: [see (editor, volume, page)].

The following is an alphabetical list of the abbreviations I have used for the editions Trollope read:

B	-Baldwyn	H	-Heywood
BF	-Beaumont & Fletcher	J	-Jonson
C	-Child	Mar	-Marlowe
De	-Dekker	Mars	-Marston

Di	-Dilke	Mas	-Massinger
F	-Ford	Mi	-Middleton
Do	-Dodsley	O	-Otway
G	-Greene	P	-Peele
Ha	-Hawkins	Sh	-Shakespeare
		S	-Shirley

Baldwyn, ed. *The Old English Drama: A Selection of Plays from the Old English Dramatists.* 2 vols. London: Hurst, Robinson, and Co., 1825.

Beaumont, Francis, & Fletcher. *The Works of Beaumont & Fletcher.* Notes by Rev. Alexander Dyce. 11 vols. London: Edward Moxon, 1843-46.

Child, Francis James, ed. *Four Old Plays.* Cambridge: George Nichols, 1848.

Dekker, Thomas. *The Dramatic Works.* 6 vols. London: John Pearson, 1873.

Dilke, Charles Wentworth, ed. *Old Plays; Being a Continuation of Dodsley's Collection.* 6 vols. London: Rodwell and Martin, 1816.

Dodsley, Robert, ed. *A Collection of the Old English Plays.* 12 vols. London, 1825-27.

Ford, John. *The Works of John Ford.* Ed. by William Gifford and Rev. Alexander Dyce. 3 vols. London: James Toovey, 1869.

Greene, Robert. *The Dramatic Works of Robert Greene.* Ed. by Rev. Alexander Dyce. 2 vols. London: William Pickering, 1831.

Hawkins, Thomas, ed. *The Origin of the English Drama.* 3 vols. Oxford, 1773. [The Folger has only vol. I.]

Heywood, Thomas. *The Dramatic Works.* 6 vols. London: John Pearson, 1874.

Jonson, Ben. *The Works of Ben Jonson.* 9 vols. London: Bickers and Son, 1875.

Marlowe, Christopher. *The Works of Christopher Marlowe.* Ed. by Rev. Alexander Dyce. 3 vols. London: William Pickering, 1850.

Marston, John. *The Works of John Marston.* Ed. by J. O. Halliwell. 3 vols. London: John Russell Smith, 1856.

Massinger, Philip. *The Plays of Philip Massinger.* Ed. by William Gifford. 4 vols. 1805.

Middleton, Thomas. *The Works of Thomas Middleton.* Notes by Rev. Alexander Dyce. 5 vols. London: Edward Lumley, 1840.

Otway, Thomas. *The Works of Thomas Otway.* 2 vols. London: J. Tonson, 1712.

Peele, George. *The Works of George Peele.* Notes by Rev. Alexander Dyce. 2 vols. London: William Pickering, 1828.

Shakespeare, William. *The Works of Shakespeare.* Revised by Alexander Dyce. 2nd ed. 9 vols. London: Chapman and Hall, 1866-67.

Shirley, James. *The Dramatic Works and Poems.* Notes by W. Gifford and Rev. Alexander Dyce. 6 vols. London: J. Murray, 1833.

A full citation for each edition is given at the beginning of Trollope's comments from that edition. Trollope's comments are given by edition and the editions are arranged in alphabetical order, just as they are listed above.

Trollope's comments are reproduced as they appear in the volumes. His spelling and punctuation, with two exceptions, have been preserved: (1) Trollope's frequent misspelling *peice* has been silently corrected, and (2) the double hyphen (=) or dash (==) has been replaced by a single hyphen (-) or dash (—). Trollope frequently omits apostrophes, and to avoid a plethora of "sic's," I have silently copied his text. When I am not sure of a word, I follow my suggestion with [?]. In a few places the handwriting is completely illegible, and I have stated so in square brackets. I have used one format for the dates (though Trollope used several forms): day month year. Trollope usually put the date at the end of a comment, but sometimes he added to the comment, and, of course, left the date where it was. I have preserved the original position of the date.

When the dates for reading a single play have been at variance, I have, where possible, relied on internal evidence and/or on Trollope's marginal record of his reading found in Halliwell's *Dictionary of Old English Plays.*

Sometimes Trollope indented the first paragraph of a comment and sometimes he did not; I have placed all the first paragraph openings flush with the left margin and have then indented subsequent (if any) paragraphs.

Though I offer here only the end comments in their entirety, I have preserved a representative sample of Trollope's random marginal comments. These are given, in square brackets and quotations marks, at the end of the appropriate play commentary.

I have preserved, in both Appendices A and B, the spelling of a title as it appears in the play edition(s) Trollope followed (when there are two different spellings, I have used the simpler). In attributing authorship, I have also followed the editors Trollope was reading. Where these attributions differ from those given by W. W. Greg in *A Bibliography of the English Printed Drama to the Restoration* (4 vols. London: The Bibliographical Society, 1962) or E. K. Chambers in *The Elizabethan Stage* (4 vols. Oxford: Clarendon, 1967), I use a
qestion mark in square brackets
[?] following the name in Appendices A and B and in Dodsley and Hawkins.

TROLLOPE READING OLD DRAMA
An Introduction and Overview

It is impossible to say how many plays Anthony Trollope attended or how much drama criticism he actually read, but we do know that between 1866 and 1882 Trollope read more than two hundred and seventy Elizabethan and Jacobean plays (including Shakespeare) — often more than once — and that he made extensive notes in his own copies.[1] These comments, written carefully in the margin and at the end of the plays in ninety-six of the one hundred and thirty volumes now owned by the Folger Shakespeare Library in Washington, D.C., provide fascinating reading for anyone interested in how a determinedly individualistic, gifted Victorian novelist reacted to Elizabethan and Jacobean drama.

Trollope's persistence in reading so many plays over so long a period is remarkable, though thoroughly characteristic of the man who undertook other enormous literary projects such as a History of World Literature[2] and a history of prose fiction[3] and who kept such meticulous records of his progress both with his recreational reading[4] and with his professional writing.[5] His judgments on the plays were probably formed through a variety of ways — childhood drama games at Julians,[6] his own theatre attendance,[7] his attempts at writing plays,[8] literary friendships at the Garrick and Athenaeum clubs, contemporary drama criticism in the press, his extensive library holdings on early drama criticism,[9] his close relationship with George Henry Lewes (who even addressed his epistolary introduction to *On Actors and the Art of Acting* to Trollope)[10] — we only know for certain that he said himself he read the plays out of "curiosity in searching their plots and examining their characters"[11] and that he prided himself on covering a great many of them before his death. He writes this in 1876: "If I live a few years longer, I shall, I think, leave in my copies of these dramatists, down to the close of the time of James I, written criticism on every play. No one who has not looked closely into it knows how many there are" (367).

No matter what public or private avenues formed Trollope's taste and judgments and no matter what use Trollope made of the plots and characters he found, readers of the drama criticism itself will find it pointed and insightful as well as satisfyingly Trollopian, familiarly definite and bluff. The Trollope who emerges from the marginalia is wonderfully consistent with the robust novelist who strode through the woods swinging his cane as he laughed and cried over his characters.[12] In his private reading, the characters of the old drama were also alive for him, and his opinions about them and about their creators are expressed vigorously. Trollope rails against inadequate editorship or against lewdness; he praises control of poetry and verse; most of all, he scrutinizes and then judges plots and characters.

Perhaps the most obvious Trollopian feature of the marginalia is the massive amount of reading it required. All of Trollope's major undertakings — whether it was writing dozens of three-volume novels or setting up postal systems in the far reaches of the globe — show his prodigious energy. Trollope went at the play reading and annotating, too, with verve; after 1866 he read on work days and holidays, year in, year out, except when deadlines loomed or when he was off to America or Ceylon or South Africa (he evidently took Shakespeare with him when he travelled to Australia in 1871 and again in 1875).[13] A couple of his lines on Jonson, penned on Christmas day of 1875, are a good example of Trollope's energy and self-irony throughout the marginalia. He has just finished what he believes to be a poor play, but instead of ignoring or dismissing it, he faithfully records his lengthy criticism and then wryly concludes: "But criticism on Cynthia's Revels is wasted. The work will have no future readers, unless it be some additional Editors or determined idler like myself" (J, II, 362).[14] "Determined," indeed!

But students of drama criticism as well as students of Trollope and his novels should find Trollope's reactions to the chief Elizabethan and Jacobean dramatists valuable. There is much to be learned in analyzing the literary taste and moral judgment implicit in Trollope's drama notes: he puts Shakespeare in a class by himself; he faults playwrights who could not paint realistic or admirable women; he prefers the rough and ready plays of the Tudors to either the more skilled but obscene or artificial Elizabethans or the convoluted Jacobeans; he prizes the language of Massinger; he admires the ingenuity but despises the lewdness of Beaumont and Fletcher; he demands that plays show excellence in plot, character, language, and something he calls sympathy; he chooses a play about women, by a forgotten playwright, as the closest to one by Shakespeare that he finds; he battles with editors' opinion or partiality.

Trollope makes numerous comments on editors and editing throughout the play volumes. Some of these are in the form of ticks, question marks, exclamation points, or brief phrases in the margins of the plays themselves, of introductory material, or of footnotes. In the end com-

14

ments on the plays Trollope referred directly to a few of the editors, and I have given examples of three (mild) criticisms of Dyce and Dodsley in this introduction. (He finds Dyce a foolishly fond critic of Webster and he criticizes Dyce's apparent underestimation of Peele's *Arraignment of Paris* just as he later faults Dodsley for underestimating Habington's *The Queen of Arragon*.) With the editor William Gifford, however, Trollope's tone is not mild. He read Gifford's editions of Ford (edited with Dyce), Shirley (also edited with Dyce), Massinger, and Ben Jonson. Some comments on the editing of Massinger are sharp, but there is anger and disgust in most of his remarks on Gifford's editing of Jonson. For example, he calls Gifford "so cross-grained a critic of critics" (J, V, 161), and says this of Gifford's footnotes: there "never was such far-fetched nonsense as in some of these notes of Gifford" (J, IV, 445), and accuses Gifford of "angry partisan denunciations" (J, I, cxcii-cxciii). How typical of Trollope that he did not skip the irritating commentary, but read every bit of it while continuing to tick, exclaim, and fume.

In this monograph I have reproduced Trollope's end comments. He made many ticks and used many exclamation marks throughout the pages of the plays, and reproducing these incidental notes would mean, in some cases, reproducing the plays themselves. Nevertheless, the import of the ticks and occasional comments is not lost because Trollope himself, in the end comment for a play, usually referred to those passages he considered most important. Frequently he copied into the end comment lines he had marked in the play. In order to give a useful and accurate picture of Trollope's marginalia, I have included some representative marginal notes. Occasionally Trollope does more than tick or use one interjection, such as "Oh!"; occasionally he wrangles with an editor or with an interpretation of a line (and then makes no mention of his disagreement in the end comment), or sometimes he marks a borrowing from Shakespeare, or even offers some gratuitous embellishment to the text. I have reproduced or summarized several of these revealing, random remarks in square brackets following the appropriate play commentary. Nevertheless, the end comments, on their own, give a full picture of the quality and substance of Trollope's commentary.

Trollope borrowed to a surprising degree from Elizabethan and Jacobean drama; he alluded to and quoted from Shakespeare frequently,[15] and it is obvious to most readers that he enjoyed a heightened sense of scene and dialogue the drama reading would have encouraged and nourished. It is not surprising, then, to find in the drama criticism the preoccupations of the novelist — particularly an interest in the handling of women characters. Throughout the marginalia, Trollope's standards

15

are those of a practised writer — are the characters well drawn? Is the language convincing and appropriate? Are the scenes properly handled? Is the poetry sustained? He judges the playwrights by his interests and faults those (such as Jonson and Fletcher) who cannot create real, honest, or virtuous women. While Shakespeare is the touchstone for excellence in language, form, and characterization, Trollope's own code of ethics establishes the moral measure for the plays.

Trollope's notes on several plays by each (read in no apparent order) show just how he judged not only Shakespeare, Fletcher and Jonson, but also Beaumont, Thomas Heywood, Middleton, Massinger, Ford, Shirley, Marston, Dekker, Marlowe, Chapman, Lyly, Peele, Greene, Kyd, and Webster. Comments on numerous plays by other less well-known playwrights in the collections of Dodsley, Baldwyn, Hawkins, and Dilke round out our understanding of Trollope the novelist drama-critic. Without here judging his taste or analyzing the possible background for his opinions, let us first look at what Trollope himself has to say about the plays he was reading from 1866 to 1882 (while he was writing twenty-seven of his own novels), and then let us look briefly — at the end of this introduction — at Trollope's evident concern with women characters.

An Overview of the Commentary

The exact order in which Trollope read the plays is chronicled in Appendix B. Here let us review first Trollope's notes on Shakespeare — since he used his plays as the standard by which to judge all others — and then Trollope's notes on the other playwrights in order by the number of plays Trollope read by them. After Shakespeare, we will begin with Beaumont and Fletcher (he read fifty-three plays by them) and end with William Habington's *The Queen of Arragon*, the single play Trollope judged most Shakespearean of all the non-Shakespearean plays he read and which I comment on further in "Trollope and the Women of the Old Drama," below.

Trollope runs out of superlatives when he praises what he consideres to be the best of Shakespeare's plays. He calls *Macbeth* "the finest play of Shakespeare" (Sh, VII, 98) but says that *Hamlet* is "the greatest work of man" (Sh, VII, 211) and says of *King Lear* "There is nothing, perhaps, in the whole range of poetry to exceed the finest passages of Lear ..." (Sh, VII, 346) but also calls *Othello* "one of the grandest works of human genius" (Sh, VII, 470). Further, he says that Imogen is "the sweetest wife in all poetry" (Sh, VII, 735), that "There is no better reading" than *The Merchant of Venice* (Sh, II, 416), and that *As You Like It* is, perhaps, the "prettiest comedy that ever was written in any language" (Sh, III, 77). Trollope delights in Falstaff, particularly in *The Merry Wives of Windsor* (Sh, I, 417) and read the two parts of *Henry IV* "a score of times" because he has "relished their fun" (Sh, IV, 402). It is obvious that Trollope has recorded the comments in Dyce's edition after years of familiarity with the plays (with the exception of *Pericles*) and we hear in all of these comments as in all the play commentary his admiration for Shakespeare's poetry and knowledge of human nature.

Yet Trollope also finds fault. For example, he thinks *The Tempest* is over-rated (Sh, I, 236); he is disgusted by the morality in *Measure for Measure* (Sh, I, 521-22) and *All's Well that Ends Well* (Sh, III, 286) and with Cressida in *Troilus and Cressida* (Sh, VI, 130); he thinks parts of *Love's Labour's Lost* "tedious" (Sh, II, 236); finds the three parts of *Henry VI* flat (Sh, V, 320); he wonders at the "bloodthirsty" confusion at the end of *Romeo and Juliet* (Sh, VI, 474) and *Hamlet* (Sh, VII, 211); and he finds parts of *The Taming of the Shrew* distractingly "far-fetched" (Sh, III, 179).

Throughout the comments on Shakespeare, Trollope is concerned with what makes good reading as opposed to good acting. He comments freely on Shakespeare's handling of story and language, and he marvels at the poet's insight into personality and motive. Perhaps the most unexpected comment Trollope makes on Shakespeare is this one on Brutus, "perhaps the finest character ever drawn by Shakespeare" (Sh, VI, 687). Overall, however, the comments on Shakespeare confirm what most of Trollope's other writing suggests about the novelist's taste and standards.

Trollope read more plays by Beaumont and Fletcher than by any other dramatists. Interestingly enough, of the fifty-three read between 1866 and 1882, forty-two were read during 1874 (sixteen of them while he was writing *The Prime Minister*). Through his years of reading, his comments on Beaumont and Fletcher are consistent, and his praise and condemnation of them characterize the standards of his drama criticism generally. His lengthy note on *The Women's Prize; or The Tamer Tamed* is a good example of Trollope's reasoning and disapproval and is worth reproducing here in full:

One cannot speak of the Tamer Tamed without speaking also of the Taming of the Shrew, — two very bad plays though Fletcher wrote the one and Shakespeare the other. But they are in this chiefly remarkable, — as shewing the mind of the two authors, — that Fletcher's play is obscene beyond measure, whereas that of Shakespeare is comparatively free from indecency. They were both written for the same age and were, we are told, played, night

17

about, to the Court. The play of Fletchers was there the more loudly lauded; from which we may gather the prevailing taste of the age, and the great fact — undoubted by lines of Shakespeare that he was infinitely beyond his age in discerning the manliness of decency.

No doubt Fletcher's comedy has more of that great dramatic merit which I may perhaps call the power of expression 'ore rotundo.' [with a round mouth] This is throughout all their works the power which has been most active in giving glory to B & F, and which has mostly made the Elizabethan dramatists, — always with the exception of Shakespeare, — the men they are. But this play of *The Woman's Prize or the Tamer Tamed*, has to my judgement three fatal faults. It is most nasty in its language; it is most absurd in its incidents; and it is most untrue to human life. In regard to the first always we must presume that the author understood his audience, — still wondering at the stage of virility which was pleased that women on the stage, (or men dressed as women) should tickle the public by most gross bawdy, while they still flattered male spectators by rigid propriety of personal conduct.

As to the second charge, it must be admitted that in all ages that have known a stage absurdity of incident has hardly been accounted a fault when producing strength of dramatic position [?]. It may be conceived that all parts in the Tamer Tamed were capable of dramatic action. As to its untruth to human life, — we are bound to acknowledge that truth to human life had not, up to the time of Fletcher, been acknowledged a virtue in English literature. At any rate it was not so acknowledged in that age. This virtue was endured in Shakespeare, — and was probably neither perceived nor criticized. No doubt it has been the virtue, which, beyond all other, has made him familiar to later English readers. With Fletcher English readers are not familiar (BF, VII, 95).

The points here on decency, plot control, truth to life, and characterization are mentioned frequently throughout the drama criticism. It is typical, too, to use Shakespeare as the standard for judging the weaknesses of the playwright. Perhaps most characteristic of the criticism and most familiar to readers of Trollope's letters is the tone of authority, and the slight irascibility beneath the controlled words.

Shakespeare appears again with *The Humorous Lieutenant*: "Fletcher as a dramatist was no doubt infinitely superior to Beaumont, and would rank, of his time, next to Shakespeare, had he not too often not [sic] done his work in such hot haste as to have missed the excellence of which he was capable" (BF, VI, 538). The fault of *Bonduca, Love's Pilgrimage* and *The Sea-Voyage*, Trollope says, is that though they have some excellent points they are either too close to or cribbed from Shakespeare (BF, V, 102/XI, 323/VIII, 370).

The lewdness that made him condemn *The Tamer Tamed* also made him disparage *The Scornful Lady, The Coxcomb, A Wife for a Month, The Captain* ("... in some respects the most disgusting in the whole range of the (so called) Elizabethan drama" [BF, III, 327]), *Women Pleased* (the love scenes are "beastly" [BF, VII, 94]), *Love's Cure*, and *The Mad Lover*. In *Love's Cure* he fears that Fletcher (he usually mentions Beaumont only to say how far superior Fletcher is to him) was often pandering to the crude tastes of the times (BF, IX, 194-95). Of those times he says (*The Coxcomb*): "In the days of Elizabeth much of the healthiness of the fun of her father's time still existed; — but in James I time men going to the theatre expected to be excited by seeing men in women's clothes act parts which no women could undertake" (BF, III, 215).

Trollope considered truth to life and realistic incident important, and he could not praise Beaumont and Fletcher for verisimilitude. However, he also believed that truth and realism should be delivered through appropriately elevated language and he does frequently commend poetic and fine passages in their plays. Of *The Woman-Hater* he says, the plots "are absurd and ill arranged" but "the language is so good, — so full of wit and humour, — that I value [?] the play" (BF, I, 99). In *The Elder Brother*, for example, Trollope praises the character Charles and his "very fine pieces of poetry" and quotes a passage to illustrate his point (BF, X, 292).

The praise Trollope does give Beaumont and Fletcher is seldom unmixed. Even in plays he considers their best, *A King and No King* and *The False One*, Trollope points out the unevenness of language, incident, or character. Of Arbaces in *A King and No King* he says: "In scene after scene the fire of the man's temper is maintained. The love of the king for his sister of course shocks us; but the readers horror at the contemplated incest is allayed by the well expressed horror of the man at his own suggested sin. The women's characters are weak, and the last scene is hurried and ineffective" (BF, II, 347). He considers *The False One* a fine play, but the "specimen of didactic wisdom" (BF, VI, 306-07) he praises most in it, he attributes to Massinger.

Throughout the comments on the fifty-three plays, Trollope becomes reconciled to Beaumont's and Fletcher's plots, to their occasional lewdness, to their love for rattling comedy; but he can seldom sympathize with their attempts to create women. He applauds much of *The Wild-Goose-Chase*, calling it "an excellent play, full of wit, with much language almost worthy of Shakespeare, — indeed more like Shakespeare's comedy than anything I now remember of Fletcher's." Yet he continues, "It is hardly necessary to say that the wit put into the womens mouths is

19

masculine and lewd. Such is always the case with Fletchers women, and more so with those of Beaumont" (BR, VIII, 206). For Trollope, this distortion of female character was unforgivable.

Trollope's opinion of twenty Thomas Heywood plays is more sharply divided than is his general assessment of the works of Beaumont and Fletcher. He found Heywood capable of some "egregiously bad" (H, II, 423) plays and also of some marvels. He believed that Heywood's work was frequently marred by haste. Of *A Challenge for Beauty* Trollops says: "The plot, or two plots, of this play are irregular and impossible, but there is some fine poetry and the reader feels that he has something to satisfy him. This is generally the case with Thomas Heywood when he works in a hurry" (Di, VI, 424). *The Faire Maid of the West* is "spoilt by too much haste" (H, II, 332). Similarly, he dismisses *A Mayden-head Well Lost* with "A worse play never was planned or written" (H, IV, 164). Ten years earlier, in 1870, he has said of *The Rape of Lucrece*, "This play is thoroughly bad & weak and the wonder is that any critic should say as much for it as is said above. The character of Lucrece is tame & priggish beyond belief..." (B, I, iv). But he did find aspects of Heywood to praise, saying also in 1870, "There is very much excellent poetry in Love's Mistress, and, it is perhaps as good a burlesque as there is in the language. It is no doubt the best work we have of Heywood" (B, II, xxiv). His highest commendation of Heywood comes in 1879 when he completes *The Four Ages* (*The Golden Age, The Silver Age, The Brazen Age,* and *The Iron Age* [in two parts]): "I look upon Heywoods Ages as one of the marvels of literature" (H, III, 432).

There are curious gaps in Trollope's schedule of reading Heywood's plays. He samples them in 1870, puts them aside until 1873, reads six in 1879, and reads another six in 1880. Evidently Heywood is a playwright Trollope was able to put aside without dismissing. It is this kind of dogged reading that makes one wonder if Trollope had some special scheme in mind for his notes (possibly an edition of his own or a commentary).

As with Beaumont and Fletcher, Shakespeare figures conspicuously, too, in the notes on the nineteen plays Trollope read by Middleton. In the notes on *The Mayor of Quinborough*, Trollope says: "This play is very hard reading, but is interesting as shewing what a gallemafrey [sic] a plot was pleasing to the frequenters of theatres in the reign of James I," And at the end, he adds, "Middleton constantly cribs from Shakespeare, and always does it badly, — Perhaps of all the so called Elizabethan dramatists he was the worst" (Do, XI, 183). Even more revealing is this observation occasioned by *Blurt, Master Constable*: "From the days of Marlowe and

Shakespeare downwards the dramatists gradually fell from poetry and charm of characters — pointing to quaintness of language and intricacy of plot, garnished with bawdry, till at last they brought plays to the path so garbled in language and so confused in incident as to be almost unintelligible to the reader of the present day. Middleton, who was late among the lot, was about the most offensive" (Mi, I, 308). There is one moment of partial praise in the readings, for when Trollope comments on *Women Beware Women*, he says: "The execution of the 3 first acts of this play is so good as to make the critic feel that Middleton, had he given himself fair chance by continued labour, might have excelled all the Elizabethan dramatists except Shakespeare." The comment, however, continues: "But the plot is so detestable, there not being a single part which is not abhorrent to the reader, that the same critic is driven to acknowledge that, with all his power of language, the author could never have become a great poet" (Mi, IV, 635). After commenting on nine of the plays, Trollope finally says this in 1877 when reading *A Chaste Maid in Cheapside*: "Middletons plays are all bad to me. The system on which he plans them disgusts me. Every character here is vitious, — except that of the girl Moll, who consequently has little to do. And then his sudden repentances are as bad as his successful rascals. But all this is not the worst. When he is funny, — in prose, — his fun is always dull. When he rises to poetry — or attempts to rise, he cannot get his feet off the ground" (Mi, IV, 88). Exactly one year later, on 31 March 1878, Trollope gives this assessment of *A Fair Quarrel*: "This is a very good play, but surely Middleton never wrote it....Middleton only understood the appetite of his audience for low buffoonery" (Mi, III, 549).

One month later Trollope combines elements of praise and condemnation in his assessment of the familiar *The Changeling*:

> There is much movement in this play and there are scenes of interest. But it is so confused and inconsequent that the reader can too readily perceive the quick unnatural way in which the dramatists of James I looked into the plots which fell in their way. There is, however, more good work in this play than ever came from Middleton's hands (Mi, IV, 300).

Trollope is not so uniformly hard on Jonson as he is on Middleton. When Trollope uses Shakespeare as the touchstone for Jonson's eighteen plays, he finds Jonson wanting, but gives some praise: "It would perhaps be unfitting to call Sejanus a fine tragedy, but it contains more of tragic poetry than anything I know in the English language out of Shakespeare; and has more matter in it, than, perhaps, any play written by Shakespeare." He completes the comparison by observing: "The cleverness [?]

of Jonson's mind and the strength of his intelligence has perhaps been somewhat kept in abeyance by the infinitely greater sweetness and perspicacity of Shakespeare's verses, and by that great man's better command of words" (J, III, 152).

Jonson's greatest power, Trollope claims, is in presenting the rural scene. In the comment on *The Sad Shepherd* Trollope summarizes his assessment of both the editor, Gifford, and Jonson: "To say that the Sad Shepherd, had it come to us entire, would have been a poem superior 'to the proudest effort of dramatic genius which time has bequeathed us' is an absurdity that could have come only from Gifford, — ....As I have before been led by certain of the poets songs, so am I now induced by this piece, to think that dramatic description of rural charm, of rural life, and of scenery, — also of rural fun and joke, was Jonsons greatest power" (J, VI, 288).

This happiness with rural themes was, for Trollope, offset by three major flaws in Jonson's technique: pride in borrowing, failing plots, and unrealistic women. The third, in Trollope's eyes, was the greatest failing. Trollope might find other playwrights who loved to borrow, others who could not sustain plot, but he seemed to find no other — not even Beaumont and Fletcher — who displeased him so much as Jonson did with his travesties of women. In *The Alchemist* he says: "Jonson never achieves a woman's part. He hardly even tries to make a woman charming. They are all whores or fools — generally both" (J, IV, 181). In *Catiline*, which Trollope calls "The heaviest play I know in the English language," Trollope attacks Jonson's females: "Jonson has endeavoured to enliven the learning of his play by the characters of Fulvia and Sempronia. He is never fortunate with his women — These are nasty, — and the reader is thankful that he has but little of Fulvia who reeks from a brothel" (J. IV, 336). And finally of the heroine in *The Devil is an Ass*, "The author has again failed in the woman's part, as he does always. She is half-whore at first, and after that she is nothing" (J, V, 148-49).

Perhaps the most remarkable feature in the notes on Jonson is Trollope's dogged rereading of him. It is evident from his notes on the seventeen plays he read in 1875 and 1876 that Trollope had no special fondness for Jonson, and yet he rereads them in 1882 (the last year of Trollope's life). He read *The Alchemist* twice, once in January 1882 and once in May; the *Poetaster* in July; and *Volpone* twice in August. His opinions do not change substantially, and yet he rereads and makes more notes. In his 1876 comment on *The Alchemist* Trollope criticizes its borrowing, its women, and Gifford's injurious "wide-mouthed praise" (J, IV, 182). In January of 1882, he finds *The Alchemist* clever and amusing, but still finds fault with the women, the plot, and its general tendency to be "... dirty, vulgar, and disgusting without ceasing for one act, one scene, one passage, or one line. Filth was common to the dramatists of James I, but here there is nothing but filth" (J, IV, 182). Finally, in May, he feels compelled to write: "I have again read the play, now for the third, or probably fourth time, and I cannot much alter the criticism written 1876. As a play it is not dramatic. As a narrative it is hardly poetic" (J, IV, 183). Comments on *Poetaster* and *Volpone* are also consistent. It is curious yet typical that Trollope felt obliged not only to reread Jonson, but to record his opinions faithfully, if repetitively.

There is an entirely different kind of energy in his reading of Massinger. He records his comments on one play in 1870, and reads another seventeen plays in March, April, June, July and August of 1876. The reason for the persistence in 1876 is fully explained in the high praise he gives Massinger's work generally, though his assessment of the one play in 1870 gives us no idea why he waited another six years to record further comments. At any rate, the eighteen commentaries on Massinger stress the same strengths and weaknesses. The comment on *A New Way to Pay Old Debts* is typical in its mixture of praise and criticism, and special in its commendation of Massinger's characterization. Most of the laudatory remarks deal with language, while the fault-finding concentrates on failures with story and character. In 1870 when he reads *A New Way to Pay Old Debts*, Trollope says: "This is an excellent play, — hardly to be called a comedy, as all that is of fine quality in it is tragic in its element. The comic character of Greedy is very poor and monotonous. The character and excellence of the play hangs almost entirely on the great strength of Overreach. I know no personage in the British drama better adapted to bring out the power of a great dramatist" (Mas, III, 590).

In 1876 when he apparently returned to Massinger's work, Trollope notes Massinger's chief weakness: "He usually falls away at the end of his plays, — not allowing himself sufficient time for elaboration" (Mas, II, 231). But perhaps his summary of Massinger's part in *The Virgin-Martyr* really best indicates his assessment: "The poetry in this play is most beautiful. The story-telling is execrable. Such may be said of much of the work of Massinger and his contemporaries" (Mas, I, 121). Of *The Bondman*, Trollope says: "To my taste the beauty of this play consists entirely in the language, the beauty and cadence of which is so great that in the mere gift of ear I am inclined to think that Massinger beat all the dramatists of his time. In the plot I can acknowledge nothing to be good.... But the melody of his words is marvellous" (Mas, II, 117).

The highest praise he could give Massinger, as with any dramatist, is to compare his work favourably with Shakespeare's. With *The Great Duke of Florence*, Trollope finds fault but does say: "... the language of this play is so good, and the poetry in many places is deliciously sweet as to make me feel inclined to place it first after Shakespeare of all the plays of the great era to which it belongs" (Mas, II, 520). To say that a dramatist approaches Shakespeare in even one aspect means praise indeed from Trollope.

Trollope can praise Ford only for occasional grandness of design or language in the nine plays he reads, and he faults him for heavy-handedness, pomposity, and a general lack of humour. The most interesting remark he makes, apart from those on language and design, has to do with morality. Of *'Tis Pity She's a Whore* he declares: "The most striking fault of the piece is that the plot does not at all require that the 'whore's' lover should be her brother. The incest is added on as a makeweight to atrocities which certainly required no such addition. Nothing in fiction, prose or poetry, disgusts so much as unnecessary crime" (F, I, 208). Trollope identifies Ford's weaknesses and strengths most forcefully in his notes on *The Lady's Trial*: "The plot is beyond measure ridiculous. There is no reason for anything that is done. But then the characters are well-handled, the language is good, there is much real poetry, and the comic parts are not grossly offensive as they are so generally with the dramatists of James I" (F, III, 98).

Trollope is slightly more generous with Shirley's nine plays than he is with Ford's. He claims that *The Young Admiral* is good in its first three acts and then is marred by Shirley's haste. Trollope praises *The Grateful Servant* for its fine language, but faults its morality:

> The idea that it was a good thing to give up to another a lady who was truly loving and truly loved, because that other was a duke is a wretched thought. The idea, too, of rescuing Lodwick from vice by the proposed offer to him of the old tutor's young wife, the offer being made jointly in most libidinous language by both husband & wife, is detestable, and could only have been possible while men took women's parts.... But all these faults were the faults of the taste of the age rather than of the poet (S, II, 93-94).

Trollope's disapproval, couched as it is in his condemnation of the age rather than the dramatist, is a reminder that he had read widely in the period and was constantly putting individual works into perspective. Though Shirley seems more favoured than Ford, he is not one of the most highly commended of the eighteen principal playwrights Trollope analyzes, at length, over some years.

Marston does not fare so well as Shirley; for Trollope, he is almost dismissible. The few plays he reads are uniformly condemned, and this condemnation continues from 1867 through 1879, when he reads his seventh and (presumably) last Marston play. He did believe that Marston could be clever in a coarse way, but he more often comments on the confusion of language and the faultiness of plots. For the last play he reads, *The Tragedie of Sohphonisba*, he gives a modicum of praise, but even here we find strict qualifications: "This, the finest of Marston's plays, has so much of true [two words illegible] poetry, as to entitle it to the name of great work. But it is often unintelligible; and sometimes so ill composed as to leave the idea that the author did not himself always know what he intended to express" (Mars, I, 215).

With seven of Dekker's plays, Shakespeare again provides the measure. *The Honest Whore* is "remarkable for its force" and "I know no play of the time in which there is a more continued flavour stolen from Shakespeares" (Di, II, 91). He admires some of the plays for their richness of language, and he admires Dekker himself for his spirit in answering Jonson's *Poetaster*; nevertheless, in the main, Trollope's comments on Dekker are negative. He dismisses *The Kings Entertainment Through the City of London* as "a thing impossible to read" (De, I, 326), and he calls *The Wonder of a Kingdom* "a most ridiculous play, made up as it were of the leavings of other plays, — half a dozen scraps of plots . . . the very omnium-gatherum of an overdone playwright" (Di, III, 98).

Trollope both condemns and praises seven plays by Marlowe. He dismisses *Edward II*, but though he finds fault with *The Jew of Malta*, he sees something worthy in it: "But there is a certain power of language which carries the reader on . . ." (Mar, I, 349). Trollope's peculiar mixture of praise and blame is found most forcefully in his 1868 comment at the end of the *Second Part of Tamburlaine the Great*:

> The first & second parts of Tamburlaine are I think the finest of Marlowe's work. The magnificence of the language is often so great as to cast into shadow the terrible defects of sentiment, & the roll of the poetry is often so fine as to convince the reader of the presence of something sublime. But as these plays are finer than the others, so are they more turgid; and there is in them the same absence of all sweetness which renders every work of Marlowe harsh. There is nothing of love, — & seldom a single character with whom the reader can sympathise. In Tamburlaine there is not one (Mar, I, 226).

When he comments on *The Massacre at Paris*, Trollope says: "As a rule Marlowe's ear is correct, and his versification though monotonous is sonorous" (Mar, II, 359).

Trollope's comments on four Chapman plays are hardly favourable. Chapman, he claims, was in too much of a hurry to produce fine work, though he does in *Widow's Tears* commend rapidity of action and form of language (Do, VI, 202). The 21 February 1880 assessment of *May Day: A Comedy* is typical of Trollope's remarks on Chapman's unevenness: "There is some drollery in this piece, and a certain pleasantness in the willingness of Emilia to be wooed and her bashfulness under the operation; — but the play throughout is confused, and this work like that of Chapman generally, is far too hurried to be worthy of praise" (Di, IV, 114).

Trollope's assessment of four plays by Lyly is almost as negative as his analysis of Chapman. He finds *Alexander and Campaspe* far-fetched but readable and better than Lyly's "novel" (Do, II, 150). *Mother Bombie* is "exceedingly silly" (Di, I, 287), *Midas: A Comedy* is chiefly remarkable for cumbersome language (Di, I, 371), and *Endymion* is saved only by a certain prettiness of language (Di, II, 97). Lyly is quaint and dismissible.

Trollope's response to Peele's four plays is divided equally. He disparages much of *David and Bethsabe* and *Edward I* and praises *The Old Wives Tale* and *The Arraignment of Paris*. The most interesting comment is on *The Arraignment of Paris*, first for this praise.

> This is a most delightful piece of poetry and fairly merits the praise which on its behalf was given to the author by Nash, when he called Peele 'the chief supporter of pleasance now living, the Atlas of poetry,' and 'primus verborum artifex' [pioneer craftsman of words]. There is a naive domestic sweetness running through the play which quite justified the description — It must be remembered that it was written before Midsummer Night's Dream, and that the compliment to Elizabeth which comes on the reader so unexpectedly on the solving of the plot of the play, probably gave rise to, certainly was not caused by, that excellent passage 'That very time I saw, but then couldn't yet [?] — &c.

and then for Trollope's disagreement with the editor Dyce: "I cannot at all understand the preference given to David and Bethsabe. Dyce quotes Campbell's eulogy of that piece, and leaves us to imply that he agrees with it. The more that I read the less I am inclined to agree with much of the criticism on the English drama which I find from the pen of the best critical editors" (P, I, 67-68). Trollope's deference to Shakespeare and his frequent irritation with editors encourage belief that he contemplated his own edition of old drama. At any rate, Peele passes the test of excellence as a playwright who creates wonders from which Shakespeare himself may have drawn.

The Shakespeare standard again appears in Trollope's assessment of Greene's four plays. He says of *Orlando Furioso*: "There is some very fine poetry, much very bad fun, and a touch here and there of excellent bombast in this very singular piece. The poetry, which in a few passages rises so high as to make one doubt in what work of the old dramatists it is to be beaten except in Shakespeare, — in the earlier part of this work" (G, I, 53). Remarks on *Friar Bacon and Friar Bungay* put Greene's work in a different relationship to Shakespeare. In the collection of Greene's work Trollope writes "The mixture of fine poetry and of absolute nonsense in this play is very strange. The marvel is that Shakespeare should have been so infinitely above his contemporaries in imagining scenes, and in writing language, fit for after ages. Greene was no doubt a scholar and a poet; but his works are now caviar to the general" (G, I, 214).

It is appropriate here to note one of the remarkable and characteristically Trollopian aspects of the marginalia that this one comment reveals. It was Trollope's habit, all through the volumes of the plays, to refer himself back to comments on the same play he had made in an earlier edition or in another collection. Sometimes, rather than write out his comment in two places he simply says "Read _____," gives the date and refers to another volume or collection. Often, too, Trollope painstakingly copies out, from one volume to another, his own comment verbatim. He usually cross-references comments even though he has copied one directly into another collection. But every now and then in the volumes, we find some small but significant and interesting variations from one (supposedly) copied comment to another. Such is the case with *Friar Bacon and Friar Bungay*. In the Greene collection Trollope prefaced the comment quoted above with "Read Jany 4 71-See Dodsley." In Dodsley (where Trollope does not refer us to the Greene collection), Trollope writes: "The mixture of fine poetry and of absolute nonsense is very strange. The marvel is that Shakespeare should have been so infinitely above his contemporaries in arranging scenes and making language fit for after ages. Greene was no doubt a scholar and a poet; but his works are now caviare to the general" (Do, VIII, 240). The difference between "arranging scenes" and "imagining scenes" and "making language fit for after ages" and "writing language fit for after ages" is perhaps significant. The second wording, the comment produced in the Greene collection, is markedly milder and more general. The wording is too close to imagine that Trollope simply wrote the Greene collection comment from memory, and too different to imagine that he did not carefully rethink the words before he used them a second time. The change suggests what the general quality of the comments found throughout the volumes substantiates — Trollope gave consideration to every comment he wrote in the plays; even the laborious tasks of cross-referencing and reproducing comments were not purely mechanical.

Trollope leaves no end comment for *James the Fourth*, but he does comment on *The Pinner of Wakefield*: "There is much life and movement in George-a-Greene; but it by no means equals Roister Doister in nature or language; nor Gammer Gurtons needle in wit — It is free from the vulgarity of the latter" (G, II, 205). But Trollope must have been fond of Greene for it is one of his plays (*Orlando Furioso*) that he may have considered reading aloud to his family in 1879.[16]

There is no fondness for Kyd, whose three plays (we have in the Folger) he found execrable. He calls *Jeronimo* "abominable trash" (Do, III, 94) and fulminates against *The Spanish Tragedy* thus: "For tediousness, improbability, and turgid pomposity this play is probably unequalled...." Yet it is typical of Trollope's criticism that even as he condemns with vigour, occasionally with rage, he usually finds something to temper the judgment. The condemnation of *The Spanish Tragedy* finishes: "... but in its day it was popular, and there is that in the grief of the father which is not without a certain effect of pathos" (Do, III, 202).

Trollope read (at least) three plays by Webster but only the comment on *The White Devil* is of interest, and it is interesting not so much for comment on the play as for remarks on the editor and the taste of Webster's time:

> Dyce speaks with very strong admiration of this play, saying that it is eminently interesting, and asking with enthusiasm how great must have been the genius which conceived so forcible and so consistent a character as Vittoria!! I cannot accede to this, and I think that Dyce so immersed himself in Elizabethan plays, that he became, (though the best of Editors,) at the same time the most laudatory of critics.... The play has all that violence of language which with the dramatists of James I was regarded as strength (Do, Vi, 325).

The works of Shakespeare, Beaumont and Fletcher, Thomas Heywood, Middleton, Jonson, Massinger, Ford, Shirley, Marston, Dekker, Marlowe, Chapman, Lyly, Peele, Greene, Kyd, and Webster represent the bulk of Trollope's drama reading, but there are, of course, numerous individual plays and playwrights who received special attention. Notes on a few of these single plays are remarkable for Trollope's praise or for his singular observations. Throughout most of the volumes of these plays, Trollope faults or praises diction, argues or agrees with an editor's judgment, continues to use Shakespeare as a touchstone, and occasionally makes a special point about the history of some word or expression or the elements of some tradition in English drama. He remarks on Gascoigne's *Jocasta*, for example, "This is interesting as the second English play we have in blank verse and the first adaptation of a play from the Greek" (C, I, 260). On Richard Edward's *Damon and Pithias*, he points out "I doubt whether I know any other play without a female character" (Do, I, 260). He says numerous times how much he enjoys the work of the time of Henry VIII, and his preference for *Gammer Gurton's Needle* suggests that he preferred good-natured bawdry tò many of the more complex and unsympathetic plays (Do, II, 83).

Two single plays stand out in Trollope's numerous comments — both he compares favourably with Shakespeare. The first is Tomkis's *Albumazar*, about which he says: "This is an excellent comedy, full of action and good broad fun, — more than equal to the Comedy of Errors, and equal in plot and life to Twelfth Night... (though of course inferior in characters and language)" (Do, VII, 212).

The other play, Habington's *The Queen of Arragon*, is the one Trollope evidently considered the best of all the non-Shakespearean drama he read: "I am disposed to say that there is finer poetry in this play than in any other drama in the English language beyond Shakespeare. And it is kept up throughout, —" and after quoting a couple of passages to support his claim he says "But it is nearly equal throughout — almost faultless in plot sentiment & language." No other play achieves this height of praise. Trollope makes this judgment in 1879, after (at least) twelve years of reading and commenting on drama. Perhaps most telling about the man and his critical temper is the swipe he takes at the editor Dodsley immediately following the praise quoted above: "And yet no one has read it. None of those who are familiar with the names of Jonson Fletcher & Massinger have heard of Habington. His Castara is unknown. His play has crept in here, without a word of praise, by accident" (Do, IX, 410). The two parts of the commentary together show Trollope as we know him from the novels and the letters; his sensitive response to beauty is accompanied by gruff, plain speaking.

Trollope and the Women in the Old Drama

Apart from the focus on Shakespeare, the attention Trollope pays to women is the single most revealing element implicit and explicit in the drama notes and deserves some comment here. For Trollope, handling of women exposes a playwright's ability; the plays he chooses as best usually feature strong, believable women characters. Frequently, he mentions women characters in the drama notes to show how inferior a playwright is to Shakespeare. Trollope's numerous, pointed references in his own novels to Ophelia, Desdemona, Lady Macbeth, Cordelia, Juliet, Imogen, Viola, or Rosalind — not to mention his own notes on the Shakespearean plays — suggest his admiration for firmly delineated female character in drama and fiction. This admiration for Shakespeare's *women* obviously tempered his response to the creations of Shakespeare's (lesser) contemporaries.

The prominence of the women in Trollope's drama commentary naturally leads us to wonder what correspondences there are between the women characters in the plays (particularly the less well-known characters in the non-Shakespearean drama) and the women characters Trollope created in his novels.

Trollope's method of note-taking (we cannot be sure whether he is reading a play for the first time) cautions us to compare character types in the non-Shakespearean plays and in the novels rather than to argue for specific or individual borrowing. But even if we disregard the dates of the play commentaries, when we compare the plays and the novels we find that Trollope is not directly indebted to the drama for his women. Nevertheless, though Trollope did not borrow any single female character from the Elizabethan and Jacobean drama, there are impressive similarities between the types of women found in the most remarkable plays and in the women Trollope created in his best novels.

What does Trollope say directly in his marginalia about the non-Shakespearean plays' women characters? Most of the direct comments are spent condemning weak love scenes, vapid heroines, and unnaturally lewd language or conduct in women (or men dressed as women). Of the more than two hundred and forty (non-Shakespearean) play commentaries, seventy-five mention women generally or specific women directly, and of these seventy-five, only twelve comments praise the women or the dramatists' treatment of them. Nine of these twelve positive comments are so highly qualified as to be almost neutral, but the other three positive, direct comments are strong indeed.

Three non-Shakespearean women characters receive direct, high praise: Cleopatra in Beaumont and Fletcher's *The False One* (BF, VI, 306-07), Camiola in Massinger's *The Maid of Honour* (Mas, III, 107), and Celia in Beaumont and Fletcher's *The Humorous Lieutenant* (BF, VI, 538-39). Most interestingly, Cleopatra, Camiola, and Celia are women Trollope could have himself created. They are familiarly and similarly intelligent, resourceful, and attractive even if one is a shrewd sexual politician, another is a highly moral, wealthy woman who renounces her love and the world to retain honour, and the third is a shy virtuous maiden who wins her proper husband.

But the indirect comments are even more revealing than the direct ones of Trollope's overall response to the dramatists' women. The plays he chooses as the best or most readable are usually those that have remarkable, admirable, sympathetic, or realistic women: Lodowick Barry's *Ram-Alley or Merry Tricks*; Beaumont and Fletcher's *Beggar's Bush, The Humorous Lieutenant, The Noble Gentleman,* and *A King and No King*; William Habington's *The Queen of Arragon*; Heywood's *A Woman Killed with Kindness, The Golden Age, Love's Mistress*; Marlowe's *Dido, Queen of Carthage*; Marston's *Maid of Honour, The Picture,* and *A New Way to Pay Old Debts*; Peele's *The Old Wives Tale* and *The Arraignment of Paris*; Shirley's *The Traitor*; and Tomkis's *Albumazar.* Trollope does not single out the women in (most of) these plays for specific commentary, but when we read the plays, we find that it is their women who make them successful or memorable. Several of the types of women found in the plays are types Trollope also created in his novels. And the drama heroines are like Trollope's own heroines—human, strong, resolute, generous, sometimes even powerful, called upon to guide others by virtuous example.

To assess the drama women so that I could then compare them with Trollope's novel women, I read the sixty-four (non-Shakespearean) plays Trollope noted as in some way remarkable—either for their women or for something special in their characterization, language, or plot. In these sixty-four plays, few single characters can compete with Trollope's own vital women. While Trollope was reading (and recordng his reading of) old drama, he also created an impressive number of powerful, independent, admirable women: Glencora Palliser, Lady Laura Standish, Madame Max Goesler, Violet Effingham, Jemima Stanbury, Caroline Spalding, Lizzie Eustace, Lucy Morris, Lucinda Roanoke, Winifred Hurtle, Emily Lopez, Isobel Boncassen, Lady Mabel Grex, and Ayala Dormer. These convincing women of the novels do share similar strengths and values with the best of the drama women. The strong women of the novels are not just self-sacrificing, though they may be self-sacrificing; they are not just intelligent and capable; they are not just noble or resolute; they are, as are the drama women, many of these things and yet peculiarly themselves. David Aitken claims that Trollope is anti-feminist, but also says that we remember and admire the powerful women despite the apparent narrowness of their creator because Trollope's art moves the characters beyond his own prejudices: "...the best of Trollope's women — the ones we and he love best of all — remain, like

31

Glencora, such lively and assertive individuals that they will never seem to readers to be specimens of the genus girl at all, but will continue to strike us as they always have as vividly, willfully, and peculiarly themselves."[17] So it is, too, with the dramatic heroines — they transcend many of the weaknesses of the plays that hold them and of the other characters surrounding them.

The play Trollope chooses as the best (most Shakespearean) of any he reads is also the one with the greatest number of remarkable women, all of whom find sisters in Trollope's novels. After more than a decade of reading and annotating plays, Trollope discovered William Habington's *The Queen of Arragon*, which I have already mentioned above in "An Overview of the Commentary." This play has three powerful women, and Trollope's praise of the play may be read as indirect tribute to them since they dominate the whole.

The play's three exemplary but human women are the Queen herself, Floriana, the wife of the court buffoon, Sanmartino; and the court lady, Cleantha. Each is a perfect example of a kind of woman Trollope created in his novels. The Queen is the picture of honour, virtue, and resolve — she refuses to marry a very powerful nobleman, who has the sanction of the people, because she will not be forced to marry a man she does not love. She is always modest and gracious, but she is also consistently firm, believing fully in herself and in the right of her heart to choose. How many Trollope heroines stand thus against apparently implacable authority to assert their own rights? Like a Trollope heroine, the Queen, too, though Queen she is, is essentially helpless except when she flouts male authority and demands her rights. The people's favourite goes to the people to win the Queen, not to the Queen, and the disguised King of Castile claims the right to marry the Queen without really asking it. All the men prove their chivalry — and ironically underscore the helplessness of the woman — by giving up their claims to her and, finally, letting her decide for herself. Most of Trollope's women, when obdurate, are granted similar civility by the families around them. It is not surprising that the most striking passages of the play regarding the Queen's story are spoken by her noble suitors and not by the virtuous Queen herself. The best of the type, the Queen of Arragon belongs to the group of firm, emblematic women whose quiet resistance speaks best for them.

Floriana, the long-suffering wife of the foolish courtier, Sanmartino, is a good example of the self-sacrificing, self-effacing, all-forgiving woman. Sanmartino mistreats her, but she suffers him patiently. Even when she tracks him down to his proposed rendezvous with the lovely young Cleantha, Floriana forgives him with almost maternal indulgence though she will make him accountable in future. Surely there is more than a trace of this forbearance in such a character as Lucy Morris (*The Eustace Diamonds*), who loves her man even when all the world says he has behaved badly to her. Whether Floriana is called on to be as loving as Lucy is another matter.

And then there is the witty, sparkling Cleantha, who leads the idiot Sanmartino on so that she can expose him to his wife, and who refuses to pledge her love to the somber Oniante because it is so much more fun to just enjoy life and not to become tied down. Cleantha loves gaiety and laughter, but she also prizes intelligence and sincerity and at the end is ready to give up some of her frivolity to have more lasting pleasures with a loving, if sober, husband. Cleantha brings to mind all of the lively women Trollope ever created, and most memorably Isobel Boncassen, Violet Effingham, Caroline Spalding, Lady Glencora, and—in social moods—Madame Max Goesler, each of whom eventually does the right thing (according to Trollope) and marries a good, solid man who needs, if not appreciates, her superior sensitivity and abilities.

Reading Habington's beautifully worded and entertaining play is like remembering the best of Trollope's many female portraits. What Habington suggests in his light, elegant drama Trollope was able to develop more fully in the novels. Trollope evidently enjoyed the play enough to rank it first for overall excellence and near-Shakespearean quality among the hundreds he read. Did he identify its strengths with his own, one wonders?

It is reassuring to know we cannot turn to the old drama itself and unearth entire characters and interactions that are so vital in Trollope's own creations. His best women live because they are original as well as human and believable. Trollope may not have borrowed women directly from the old drama,[18] but the very vividness of his own portraits suggests that he passed through the old, crowded gallery with an eager and discerning eye.

*   *   *

If the quality of comments throughout the play volumes is consistent with Trollope's personality and with his aesthetic theories, and the method of notetaking is consonant with his love for meticulous schedules and journals, certainly his reading of the plays themselves is characteristic. He did not read straight through any volumes, but read according to some scheme of his own. Even when he read thirty-two Beaumont and Fletcher plays in a row, from June to December of 1874, he

33

did not plod straight through a collection. The reason for the order of his reading is a mystery, but the skipping about does indicate that Trollope was no more purely regimented in his critical recreation than he was absolutely faithful to his infamous 250 words per quarter hour in his novel writing (*Autobiography*, p. 272). In no matter what order he or she finds them, the reader is naturally struck by Trollope's evident delight in precise, personal commentary. Above all, the freshness and energy of the painstaking marginalia provide entertaining evidence of Anthony Trollope's hearty joy in language and character.

NOTES

¹ I am indebted to *English Studies in Canada* for allowing me to reprint this piece, which originally appeared (in a slightly different form) in their pages. © 1987 by the Association of Canadian University Teachers of English. Reprinted from *English Studies in Canada*, Vol. XIII, No. 3, September 1987, pp. 281-303, by pemission of the Association.

Trollope dates almost all of his end comments on the plays. The earliest date is 26 November 1866 and the latest is August 1882. Trollope did also read thirty-five Beaumont and Fletcher plays between 1850 and 1853. He gives the dates for his reading in the 1647 Beaumont and Fletcher Folio, which is housed in the Shakespeare Institute in Stratford-upon-Avon. See I. Ekeblad, "Anthony Trollope's Copy of the 1647 Beaumont and Fletcher Folio," *N&Q*, 204 (1959), 153-54.

² N. John Hall, "An Unpublished Trollope Manuscript on a Proposed History of World Literature," *Nineteenth-Century Fiction*, 29 (1974), 206-10.

³ Bodleian MS. Don. C. 10*, p. 96.

⁴ See N. John Hall, "Trollope Reading Aloud: An Unpublished Record," *N&Q*, 220 (March 1975), 117-18.

⁵ Bodleian MS. Don. C. 9, 10.

⁶ G. Harvey, *The Art of Anthony Trollope* (New York: St. Martin's Press, 1980), p. 12.

⁷ Trollope's familiarity with London generally would suggest theatre attendance, but I have uncovered no records. Many of the comments on Shakespeare suggest that he did see the plays. It is likely he did see performances of the plays named in his early Commonplace Book. N. John Hall, "Trollope's Commonplace Book, 1835-40," *Nineteenth-Century Fiction*, 31 (June 1976), 20.

⁸ Neither his five-act play *The Noble Jilt* (1850), nor his play *Did He Steal It?* (1869), based on *The Last Chronicle of Barset*, made it to the stage in Trollope's time.

34

9 Trollope's Library Catalogue of 1874 is in the Victoria and Albert Museum in London. Studies have been made of it and of the extensive drama holdings: A. Wright, "Anthony Trollope as a Reader," in *Two English Novelists: Aphra Behn and Anthony Trollope* (Los Angeles: University of California, 1975), 45-68; R. H. Grossman and A. Wright, "Anthony Trollope's Libraries," *Nineteenth-Century Fiction*, XXXI (1976), 48-64.

10 (London: Smith Elder, & Co., 1875), pp. v-xii.

11 *An Autobiography* (Oxford: Oxford Crown Edition; rpt. 1950), p. 367. All subsequent references will be given in the text by page number.

12 Anthony Trollope, "A Walk in a Wood," *Good Words*, 20 (1879), 595-600.

13 Compare Appendix B of this study with Michael Sadleir's schedule of Trollope's novel writing in *Trollope: A Commentary* (1945; rpt. London: Oxford University Press, 1961), pp. 406-13.

14 See KEY TO THE TEXT for an explanation of the format and the abbreviations used throughout this study.

15 See especially G. Harvey, *The Art of Anthony Trollope*. For borrowing from Shakespeare, see William Coyle, "Trollope and the Bi-Columned Shakespeare," *Nineteenth-Century Fiction*, 6 (1951), 33-46.

16 N. John Hall, "Trollope Reading Aloud," p. 118.

17 David Aitken, "Anthony Trollope on the 'Genus Girl,'" *Nineteenth-Century Fiction*, 28, 434.

18 For recent studies on Trollope's novels and the plots of some of the old plays, see G. Harvey, *The Art of Anthony Trollope* and G. Harvey, "A Parable of Justice: Drama and Rhetoric in *Mr. Scarborough's Family*," *Nineteenth-Century Fiction*, 37, 419-29.

Baldwyn, ed. *The Old English Drama: A Selection of Plays from the Old English Dramatists.* 2 vols. London: Hurst, Robinson, and Co., 1825.

(Baldwyn, I, iv-v) *The Second Maiden's Tragedy* [anonymous]

The language often fine —with many pathetic touches. The plot hopelessly absurd and grotesquely horrid —The morality bad & indeed inhuman. To attribute the play to Shakespeare would be meretricious [?]. This more like the work of Ford, but was written before Ford's time. It contains words which I had thought to be more modern than its date, —such as cathedral. 30 April 1870

Shakespeare ever uses the words Cathedral Church —never cathedral alone, as it is here used familiarly.

(Baldwyn, I, iii) *A Pleasant Conceited Comedy* [Cooke]

I cannot allow any part of the above eulogy.* The play is poor throughout, and the incidents absurd and uninteresting. 1 May 1870

[*Baldwyn (p. iii) says "This play agrees perfectly with the description given of it in the title; it is certainly a most pleasant conceited comedy, rich in humour, and written altogether in a right merry vein."]

(Baldwyn, I, iv) *The Ball* [Chapman and Shirley; compare (S, III, 91)]

A much better play than the last but very unequal. The knights and the ladies, Bostock (the common stage coward) the lord and the Colonel are very well. Freshwater is utterly deficient in fun or wit & the French dancing master not much better. The discrimination of character above spoken of* I do not discern. The two knights are as alike as two peas as are also the two ladies Hon. & Rosamund. 2 May 1870 See also Shirley's works.

[*Baldwyn (p. iv) says: "There is more nicety and discrimination in the characters than Chapman was capable of...."]

36

(Baldwyn, I, iv) *The Rape of Lucrece* [Th. Heywood; virtually identical in (H, V, 257)]

This play is thoroughly bad & weak and the wonder is that any critic should say as much for it as is said above. The character of Lucrece is tame & priggish beyond belief, nor is there a single fine line put into her mouth. The song "To give my love good morrow" is the best thing in the play p 75. [Act IV.vii] 3 May 1870

(Baldwyn, II, xxiv) *Love's Mistress* [Th. Heywood; compare (H, V, 160)]

There is very much excellent poetry in Love's Mistress, and, it is perhaps as good a burlesque as there is in the language. It is no doubt the best work we have of Heywood. 30 May 1870 It is to be observed that the author here continues to introduce a very large number of quaint mythological stories, and has sometimes done so with infinite humour.

(Baldwyn, II, x) *Albertus Wallenstein* [Glapthorne]

I have read no more than the first act of this play,—which is surely enough. The even tenor of its versification is no compensation for its coldness and want of nature. When a lover on wishing his new wife good night prays that her dreams may be free from paraphrasing 'on his memory' (see close of Act I)—his further raptures may certainly be neglected. 25 June 1870

(Baldwyn, II, xiv) *Dido, Queen of Carthage* [Marlowe and Nash; verbatim in (Mar, II, 439)]

This burlesque on Dido's story as told by Virgil is pretty, quaint, and graceful. It can hardly be called a play, though the ending be tragical enough. 26 June 1870

(Baldwyn, II, 78-79) *The Lady's Privilege* [Glapthorne]

It is impossible to handle too severely the absurdity of the plot of this play, or the ridiculous platitudes and pretentious pomposity of the language. The monstrous magnificence of the words put into Doria's mouth sometimes beat all that I have met with in the second or third rate Elizabethan writers. He describes love as

One who emblems
The glory of mortality in each look;
Contracts the orb of lustre in a glance;
!!! Brandishes beams, whose purity dispense
Light more immaculate than the gorgeous east
Wears, when the prostrate Indian does adore
Its rising brightness.

And this author's comedy, as attempted in the characters of Frangipan and Corimba is almost more contemptible than his high-flown poetry.

Nevertheless, there is an action and life in the piece which make it readable, which cannot be said for his Albertus Wallenstein. 3 July 1870

Beaumont, Francis, & Fletcher. *The Works of Beaumont & Fletcher.* Notes by Rev. Alexander Dyce. 11 vols. London: Edward Moxon, 1843-46.

(Beaumont & Fletcher, I, 99) *The Woman-Hater*

The plot, — or rather the two plots of this play are absurd and ill arranged. The characters have but little consequence or special bearing, — with the exception of Gondarino and Lazarillo who are too grotesque to be regarded as human characters. Even Oriana loses so much by her first frolic with Gondarino that she never regains respect. But the language is so good, — so full of wit and humour, — that I value [?] the play. 11 December 1873

(Beaumont & Fletcher, I, 196) *Thierry and Theodoret*

Surely nothing can be worse than this tragedy. The one [?] of Brunhault [sic] is unnatural & disgusting, & the virtue of Ordella is unnatural & insipid. The versification of that part which I suppose to be Beaumonts is flat, and in no part of the tragedy do the lines rise to the height of true poetry. Even the pathos of Ordella's fate is lost in the absurdity of the action. [No Date]

[On p. 117, Act I.ii, Trollope has written "Not poetry—but measured *lines*"]

(Beaumont & Fletcher, I, 197) *Philaster: or Love Lies A-Bleeding*

Touching Philaster there can be no doubt that there are faults in the plot so heavy as to make the play fairly open to the heaviest shafts of criticism. Dion's false evidence is such a fault. The violence of Philaster to the two women are two more such faults. And the sudden change in the king's character, — in which there is a little counter-change worse than all when he returns to threatening Arethusa, — is a third. But the poetry of the piece from first to last suffices to redeem all such faults, — and there is a touch or two of pathos which is exquisite.

> Aret. 'A little bend thy looks
> Philas.   I do.
> Areth. Then know, I must have them, — & thee'

Nothing was ever better done. [No Date]

[Beside Act I,ii, Trollope writes "Excellent" and on the next page beside Philaster's speech starting "I have a boy" he writes "Beautiful"]

(Beaumont & Fletcher, I, 425) *The Maid's Tragedy*

I cannot agree with Mr. Dyce that the play, — The Maid's Tragedy — is a great tragic effort. The story is so full of faults, that it is all faults, — and in the characters there is neither strength nor consistency. Evadne, who is the centre piece of the play—becomes a changed woman not thru repentance but at her brother's bidding — The impudence of her wickedness is at first attractive; but the fury of her unreal remorse has nothing to recommend it. Even Amintor is as base as he is weak, from his early boastings; — and is odious from his senseless rejection of Aspatia. Melantius is a mouthing Bobadil, — and to have kept up any character should have killed the king himself. The counterfeiting Aspatia is simply a poor stage trick.

So much for the play. But all these faults are redeemed in the reading by the strength of the language, & were probably redeemed in the acting by the strong life of the piece.

As a play the Maid's Tragedy cannot be too violently condemned. 26 November 1866

(Beaumont & Fletcher, II, 121) *The Faithful Shepherdess*

There is much very pretty versification in this pastoral but it is tedious and unequal. The passages quoted in the notes from Milton as having been borrowed from Fletcher, — and which undoubtedly were taken from this poem of Fletcher's, — shew the immense difference between first and second rate poetry.

Fletcher's subjective treatment of lewdness, — in which lies the very pith of the poem, — is to us in these days disgusting. Milton handles the same subject but never offends. This no doubt was in part due to the altering tastes of the times. 11 December 1873

(Beaumont & Fletcher, II, 229) *The Knight of the Burning Pestle*
Very poor. 9 March 1869

(Beaumont & Fletcher, II, 347) *A King and No King*
This is certainly a fine play; — as I think among the best which our authors wrote; in which opinion, however, I am again at variance with Mr. Dyce. It is [to] the character of Arbaces that the praise is due, a part which I am not surprised that Garrick should have desired to act. It is full of life and would give grand scope for a kingly-visaged actor. In scene after scene the fire of the man's temper is maintained. The love of the king for his sister of course shocks us; but the reader's horror at the contemplated incest is allayed by the well expressed horror of the man at his own suggested sin. The women's characters are weak, and the last scene is hurried and ineffective.

Bessus is not peculiarly attractive to me. The stage coward of the time was very common; and Bessus is inferior to either Bobadil or Parolles. 8 June 1874

(Beaumont & Fletcher, II, 449) *Cupid's Revenge*
A very bad play, — monstrously bad; — so bad as to offend one's taste in every direction; past all criticism bad, weak in its virtue, as with Leucippus, disgusting in its villainy as with Bacha, and with almost nothing of pathos; certainly with nothing of humour. Yet there are a few fine lines — as

> Yet does resemble
> Apollo as I oft have fancied him
> When rising from his bed he stirs himself
> And shakes day from his hair

— and others
But it has been written in violent haste. 17 June 1874

(Beaumont & Fletcher, II, 570) *Four Plays in One*
In these four plays there is some very fine poetry, and in these first much dramatic action. The triumph of honour is very pretty, and is wonderful as containing so excellent a plot in so small a compass. The moral of the triumph of time I cannot understand, — even with the assistance of Emanuel. 27 September 1874

(Beaumont & Fletcher, III, 113) *The Scornful Lady*

Surely this is in every respect a bad play. Yet we are told that it was very popular. It is more than ordinarily coarse for Beaumont, or even for Fletcher. There is no reason in any of the various changes. There is no character with whom the spectator can sympathise, — and no special beauty in the language. To my taste it is vulgar tedious and foolish. 17 December 1873

(Beaumont & Fletcher, III, 215) *The Coxcomb*

This is a most revolting play, — but, as regards execution, very unequal. We are told that it is the finest work of Beaumont & Fletcher. The two first acts are as bad in writing as in plot. The workmanship of Act III & IV is good. I presume that Beaumont wrote the first part, and Fletcher the last.

There are two plots, — that by which Antonio gives up his wife to his friend Mercury; and that which refers to the love of Ricardo and Viola. The first is so offensive as to make the reader wonder that it should not have offended even the taste of the age of James I. It is not only that the fool should by stratagem have got his friend to lie with his wife, but that the wife, with whom the reader is intended to sympathise should have debased herself by yielding. In truth such a plot would have been impossible 20 years before the appearance of this play. In the days of Elizabeth much of the healthiness of the fun of her father's time still existed; — but in James I time men going to the theatre expected to be excited by seeing men in women's clothes act parts which no women could undertake.

In the second story, that of Viola and her drunken lover, the reader's feelings would be all with Viola, (as they are intended to be), had not the author begun with the mistake of making her rob her father? [sic]

Many of the earlier scenes in which Viola appears are kindly [?] enough. 18 May 1874

(Beaumont & Fletcher, III, 327-28) *The Captain*

This is a most filthy play, — in some respects the most disgusting in the whole range of the /so-called/ [sic] Elizabethan drama. The horror excited by Lelia's character is so great, that it is even increased by the action of her sudden repentance. The incident, too, of the Captain being brought into the lady's arms immediately after his bath from the window is more than usually disgusting. There is very little in the language to redeem all this. The songs are the best part of the play. 4 July 1874

41

(Beaumont & Fletcher, III, 452) *The Honest Man's Fortune*

A very heavy play—in which the difference between Beaumont and Fletcher is, perhaps, as clearly seen as in any of their works. It is chiefly from the hands of Beaumont and is very dull,—lacking the craft of Fletcher, except in the malediction of Montague on the suitors which I take to be Fletcher's work. I know no play in which there is less truth of character. There is not an ounce of nature in the whole of it. Orleans, Amiens, Montague, Charlotte, Duchess, and Lamira are alike artificial and untrue. October 1874

(Beaumont & Fletcher, III, 563) *The Little French Lawyer*

A confused ill-arranged play, with very little to recommend it. The women talk bawdry in a manner that no doubt recommended it to the playgoers of James Ist's time. I do not know that there is any thing else in the piece that can have been attractive.

I should think that the name must have followed the acting of the special part,—as in Greene's Tu Quoque, and the Lord Dundreary of our own time. November 1874

(Beaumont & Fletcher, IV, 96) *Wit and Several Weapons*

This is most wretched trash. I know nothing in the dramatic work of that age so very bad. It is unlike the work of those poets in this,—that the scene is in England & the characters all English. But how inferior to some of the older plays,—even before Shakespeare. November 1874

(Beaumont & Fletcher, IV, 196) *Wit without Money*

There is much to be said for this play and the way in which the two women are won, though not suited to our ideas, was good stage comedy in the days of James I. There is much wit and some poetry. But these are all the faults of extreme haste. The language is often unintelligible, and the method of talking is the same for the high characters and for the low. As when Lance the servant says

> Maids are clocks,
> The greatest which they shew goes slowest to us
> &c.

The prettiest words in the play are spoken by Francisco to Isabel [la].

> Ladies' honours
> Were ever in my thoughts unspotted ermines,
> Their good deeds holy temples.

11 June 1874

(Beaumont & Fletcher, IV, 300-01) *The Faithful Friends*

This is a remarkable play — In the first place as being so utterly unlike Fletchers work, and, as far as I know, Beaumonts, — and secondly as containing such fine passages as to which I cannot judge who wrote them, together with a great amount of absolute trash. The plot is very absurd. The king is a villain, and yet, at last, his villainy is condoned without cause & he comes forth triumphant, leaving the punishment to the lesser villains — Or if that is not intended, then the plot is so obscure that the reader cannot follow it. The character of Philomena is very poor, — which should have been the leading character. But there are redeeming passages. And nothing in the play strikes so much as the sanctity of royalty. Take the following few lines as an example of both — Act IV Sc. iv.

> Tull.   Good sir, think,
> Although I am your subject, and do view
> Each beam that shines about you, and conceive
> How dear you are to the gods, to angels, saints,
> The world, and mankind; — though I know you are
> A temple so divine and hallowed
> That but to dream ill of you, were to plunge
> My soul into damnation; yet, to it,
> Think what this woman is; — my wife, sir, she's my wife;
> My chaste dear wife, a word that's precious,
> Self of myself, nay, such a self beyond
> That where she falls my name is perished.

November 1874

(Beaumont & Fletcher, IV, 383) *The Widow* [compare (Do, XII, 295); (cr. Mi, III, 440)]

In spite of Dyce's eulogy, I must declare this to be a very poor play. A part but only a small part of act V is, I should say, by Fletcher. The fourth act which is said to be Jonson seems to me to be hardly better than the others. The wit of it is poor wit, and the fun poor fun. There is a grotesqueness in the absurdity of putting dialogue so absolutely English into the mouths of Italians and laying the scene at Capo d'Istria. It is more thoroughly English, — ie. has kept less likeness [?] to the foreign plots from which it was borrowed, than anything of Fletcher. 30 November 1874

(Beaumont & Fletcher, IV, 494) *The Custom of the Country*

This is a most tedious play, — but in which each plot and each fragment of plot disgusts. Pepys says that the play was bad when acted, except that Knipp sang a good song in the widow's part. The only song marked in the play, is to be sung by some person not named, certainly not by the widow.

The play would have been better without the first act or any allusion to the custom of the country. The plot might have been confined to the action in Lisbon and to the pretended death of Duarte and the loves of Hippolyta. But like Fletcher's plays generally it is overdone with action, and in this piece we suffer by feeling that all the persons who are happy, fortunate and good at the end, have been abominable in the action. There is not even much good writing to reconcile us, — nothing sufficiently striking to be quoted in praise. 25 May 1874

(Beaumont & Fletcher, V, 102) *Bonduca*

An excellent play with many firstrate [sic] scenes, much humour, and a fair amount of poetry. But there is no passage that rises to any very great altitude. Perhaps the finest lines in the play are those uttered by Suetonius in praise of Caratach towards the end of the first act.

In all these plays there is much too closely copied from Shakespeare. 9 June 1874

(Beaumont & Fletcher, V, 206-07) *The Knight of Malta*

There is very much in this play to delight. The poetry often rises to a high pitch and sometimes almost equals anything written by Fletcher. The opening speech of the villain Mountferrat is a sample.

> Tempests I have subdued & fought 'em calm
> &c &c &c
> And yet I cannot conquer her bright eyes.

It is I think worthy of remark, though I have not seen it remarked elsewhere, that the last half of the last scene can hardly have been written by Fletcher, — It consists of prose measured out into lengths which was not Fletcher's fault.

The aptitude of the age for bawdry is here very conspicuous as having been specially celebrated in the characters of persons intended to be modest; — as though each should say; — "I will indulge myself to the utmost in imagination to shew more completely the strength of my self control." The poet no doubt knew that if he meant to please he must be lewd even in painting chastity. 8 December 1874

(Beaumont & Fletcher, V, 315-16) *Valentinian*

This is, certainly, a very fine play; — perhaps, in many respects, the best work of the authors. The dramatic interest is maintained throughout and the language never falls away. Perhaps the blot on the piece is the revenge at last executed by Eudoxia, for whom no one cares. Nothing can be much grander than the way in which Lucina is sent away to die. 26 September 1874

(Beaumont & Fletcher, V, 392) *The Laws of Candy*

I know no play the plot of which is more absurd than the plot of this. The condemnation of all the offenders against the laws of Candy is revolting to the critical sense. But a play might be good in spite of that. The laws might be natural. But here the attempt at passion is most unnatural. It is usual with Fletcher that men and women should fall in love at first sight, and then attempt to boast of their love as though it had been strengthened by time. This is always feeble; — but never perhaps more feeble than in reference to the love of Erota for Antinous, — a love which she is afterward enabled to abandon. The language is fairly good throughout, but never rises high. 1 November 1874

(Beaumont & Fletcher, V, 486) *The Queen of Corinth*

A very bad play; — not worth much criticism. I do not think there is a fine passage in it, and the plot is foul & uninteresting. 19 June 1874

(Beaumont & Fletcher, VI, 113) *The Loyal Subject*

A good bustling play — with some fine passages; — marred by great want of discrimination of character. The Duke is devilishly bad, or full of honour just as may suit the author's need at the moment. October 1874

(Beaumont & Fletcher, VI, 212-13) *The Mad Lover*

The character of Memnon is grand throughout. In some of the earliest scenes nothing can be happier than his madness. His grandiosity is so magnificent as to carry every thing before it. But there is a low obscenity about other parts of the play which is absolutely disgusting. 13 October 1874

I find on referring to Dyce's preface that his judgement on the character of Memnon is quite at variance with mine. But, much as I admire Dyce as an Editor, I cannot often agree with him as a critic.

(Beaumont & Fletcher, VI, 306-07) *The False One*

Certainly a very fine play. The characters of Cleopatra and Caesar are very well drawn, and here and there throughout the play there are didactic sentences of which the pith and language are equally excellent. The closeness of the translation of Lucan in some passages is very remarkably even [?] that they are well woven intò the general plot of the play, and not inserted as mere translations, as pieces out of the Satires of Horace in Jonson's Poetaster.

As a specimen of the didactic wisdom of perhaps Massinger, some words may be quoted out of the mouth of Septimius Act II Sc ii.

> I now perceive the great thieves eat the less,
> And the huge leviathans of villainy
> Sup up the merits, — nay the men and all,
> That do them service, and spout 'em out again,
> Into the air, as thin and unregarded
> As drops of water that are lost in the ocean.

December 1874

(Beaumont & Fletcher, VI, 414) *The Double Marriage*

This play certainly contains much fine poetry, — some passages almost as fine as any that Fletcher ever wrote. For instance

> Chaster than crystal on the Scythian hills, [sic, cliffs]
> The more the proud winds court, the more the purer
> > And
> Even there [sic, then] within her patient heart she locked thee,
> There [sic, Then] hid thee from the tyrant, — there preserved thee.
> > Again
> May not we yet though fortune ever divided us,
> And set an envious stop between our pleasures.
> Look thus at one another, sift and meet thus.

The plot and content of the play are good in the four first acts. The last, in which Juliana foolishly stabs Virolet is very bad. But Fletcher never had fortune to finish a play well.

The plagiarism of Sancho's banquet is ridiculous as a theft, and very badly woven into the play. 18 July 1874

(Beaumont & Fletcher, VI, 538-40) *The Humorous Lieutenant*

Of all Fletcher's comedies this surely is the best, — and perhaps of all his plays — and yet this verdict is not borne out by any criticism that I have seen of the author, for I do not find the piece spoken of with much praise. Fletcher as a dramatist was no doubt infinitely superior to Beaumont, and would rank, of his time, next to Shakespeare, had he not too often not [sic] done his work in such hot haste as to have missed the excellence of which he was capable. In the Humorous Lieutenant there are many passages which shew an amount of labour elsewhere wanting. Where is there a prettier love scene than that between Demetrius and Celia in the first act, second scene? And in what play are there finer passages or more lines worthy of quotation? Take the speech of Demetrius Act I scene i in which he asks his father to allow him also to gather his crop of laurels. And for single lines take the following, — with very many others.

> "Fortune has hours of loss, and hours of honour"
> "Our lives are but our marches to our graves."
> "And when you crown your swelling cups to fortune
> What honourable tongue can sing my story?"
> "Then when you shake in horror of this villainy,
> Then will I rise a star in heaven and scorn you."
> "I am not now Demetrius. Thou has't changed me;
> Thou woman with thy thousand wiles hast changed me."

The character of Celia is maintained throughout with magnificence of words and sentiment.

The play ends with tawdry lines as do almost all the plays of these authors. It is also too long and drags in the third & fourth acts. But taken as a whole it almost justifies the reputation which Fletcher has won and which so many of his plays cause us to consider as misplaced [?]. The humour of the Lieutenant too though very extravagant, is good humour throughout. 22 June 1874

In 1830 Dyce reprinted this play from an MSS preserved in Wales, under the name of Demetrius and Enanthe; but he only mentions this edition in the present work. In his memoirs he spoke slightingly of the piece. But Halliwell calls it "an exceedingly good play."

(Beaumont & Fletcher, VII, 94) *Women Pleased*

To my thinking a very poor play indeed. The low comedy is unnatural & foul, and the more serious parts equally unnatural and almost equally foul. I cannot agree with Dyce in calling it a very entertaining tragedy-comedy. There is nothing of tragic element in it. Nor can I agree with him when he says that the part of Penurio is original. He is the usual hungry greedy servant-;- [sic] only absurdly hungry and greedy. The made up love scenes of Isabella and her brother Claudio are beastly. 23 October 1874

(Beaumont & Fletcher, VII, 95) *The Woman's Prize; or The Tamer Tamed*

One cannot speak of the Tamer Tamed without speaking also of the Taming of the Shrew,—two very bad plays though Fletcher wrote the one and Shakespeare the other. But they are in this chiefly remarkable,— as shewing the minds of the two authors,—that Fletcher's play is obscene beyond measure, whereas that of Shakespeare is comparatively free from indecency. They were both written for the same age and were, we are told, played, night about, to the Court. The play of Fletchers was there the more loudly lauded; from which we may gather the prevailing taste of the age, and the great fact—undoubted by lines of Shakespeare that he was infinitely beyond his age in discerning the manliness of decency.

No doubt Fletcher's comedy has more of that great dramatic merit which I may perhaps call the power of expression 'ore rotundo' [with a round mouth]. This is throughout all their works the power which has been most active in giving glory to B & F, and which has mostly made the Elizabethan dramatists,—always with the exception of Shakespeare,— the men they are. But this play of The Woman's Prize or the Tamer Tamed, has to my judgement three fatal faults. It is most nasty in its language; it is most absurd in its incidents; and it is most untrue to human life. In regard to the first always we must presume that the author understood his audience,—still wondering at that stage of virility which was pleased that women on the stage, (or men dressed as women) should tickle the public by most gross bawdy, while they still flattered male spectators by rigid propriety of personal conduct.

As to the second charge, it must be admitted that in all ages that have known a stage absurdity of incident has hardly been accounted a fault when producing strength of dramatic position [?]. It may be conceived that all parts in the Tamer Tamed were capable of dramatic action. As to its untruth to human life,—we are bound to acknowledge that truth to human life had not, up to the time of Fletcher, been acknowledged a virtue in English literature. At any rate it was not so acknowledged in that age. This virtue was endured in Shakespeare,—and was probably neither perceived nor criticized. No doubt it has been the virtue, which beyond all others, has made him familiar to later English readers. With Fletcher English readers are not familiar. 4 March 1869

(Beaumont & Fletcher, VII, 303) *The Chances*

This is a very fair play, but nothing in it so good as to make me understand why it should have been kept on our stage so late as John Kembles day. He certainly prepared it for the English stage, as I have the copy cut by himself for acting. The most interesting passage in the play is that in which the man-witch, Vecchio, explains his way of acting with the people so as to carry on his trade. No doubt this was general in the days of Eliza. & perhaps of James I, —though it occasionally led to execution and death. 11 July 1874

(Beaumont & Fletcher, VII, 411) *Monsieur Thomas*

A good rattling, noisy comedy, —with no great subtlety of character or strength of purpose [?], coarse in language and in conception, —but droll enough. 16 September 1874

(Beaumont & Fletcher, VII, 513) *The Island Princess*

A fine stirring play, with much excellent poetry; —the character of Armusio very good indeed —of course there is infinite absurdity in the manipulation, certain persons being infamous murderers in one scene, and magnanimous & noble in the next. But such is the manner of Fletcher. November 1874

It is seldom that the Elizabethan dramatists rouse themselves to any great efforts on behalf of religion. Priests and things priestly are generally matter for ridicule —But Armusio, in the Island Princess, says some very fine things on behalf of Christianity.

(Beaumont & Fletcher, VIII, 99) *The Pilgrim*

I cannot agree with the praise given by Collier [?] to this play, —nor, especially, to the scene in which Roderigo suddenly becomes virtuous under the auspices of Pedro. It is unnatural, and there is nothing in the language to redeem this improbability. There are pretty passages in the play, & that is I think all that can be said for it; —the prettiest being the first lines of Act V scene IV

> How sweet these solitary places are, how wantonly
> The wind blows through the leaves and courts &
> plays with 'em! &c &c

and in the same scene

> Nothing rocks love asleep but death —

16 December 1874

(Beaumont & Fletcher, VIII, 206) *The Wild-Goose-Chase*

20 December 1873

This is an excellent play, full of wit, with much language almost worthy of Shakespeare, — indeed more like Shakespeare's comedy than anything I now remember of Fletcher's. But, as is always the case with Fletcher's plots, the scheming of the play is antagonistic to one's realistic sense, some of the plots laid by the women are irrational; and there is no reason why the wild-geese should have been caught, except that the play must end. It is a fault in the play, too, that Oriana, who is the heroine, does not interest us till the 4th act. It is hardly necessary to say that the wit put into the womens mouths is masculine and lewd. Such is always the case with Fletchers women, and more so with those of Beaumont. But Lillia-Bianca, Rosalura, Pinac, Belleur, and Mirabel are kept up with such infinite life, that the piece is charming to read, and must have charmed when acted.

(Beaumont & Fletcher, VIII, 289) *The Prophetess*

A poor play; — uninteresting and ill contrived; the language never rising to grandeur, and with no prettiness of poetry. July 1874

(Beaumont & Fletcher, VIII, 370) *The Sea-Voyage*

The sea Voyage is a confused awkward ill-arranged imitation of the Tempest, in some parts very nasty, and throughout undramatic. But there are one or two scenes between Albert and Aminta full of grace and passion and which should have saved it from Dyce's relentless censure. The plea on behalf of truth is very good Act IV sc. iii

> Oh, my best sir, take heed,
> Take heed of lies! Truth, though it trouble some minds,
> Some wicked minds that are both dark and dangerous,
> Yet it preserves itself, comes off pure, innocent,
> And, like the sun, though never so eclips'd,
> Must break in glory.

December 1874

(Beaumont & Fletcher, VIII, 494) *The Spanish Curate*

A poor play, hurried, coarse in its delineations, and with no character in it true to nature. But there is a life about it which makes it readable, and which, I can understand may have made it a good acting play. 16 October 1874

(Beaumont & Fletcher, IX, 104) *Beggar's Bush*

A very good play throughout, with excellent characters and well-sustained plot; — the fooling all good of its kind, and nothing to disgust. It must have acted very well. 27 June 1874

(Beaumont & Fletcher, IX, 194-95) *Love's Cure*

A play full of most beastly allusions, — which were not in consonance with the feeling of the age last past, but preluding the beastliness of an age to come. I fear that Fletcher was a pander to the growing bawdry of his time. And here, as elsewhere with Fletcher, — and also with Beaumont, — the idea of love is infinitely unnatural — with them it becomes at first sight — a raging passion, — as tho' one should say, though I have but seen her, I must die but I must have her. There is not, and never has been truth in such a telling of a love-story as this.

The rogues in the play are, moreover, beastly rogues.

But, nevertheless, there are fine passages in Love's Cure; as when Genevora says, act V scene iii

> 'Be 'est thou desperate
> Of thine own life? Yet, dearest, pity mine.
> Thy valour's not thine own. I gave it thee.
> These eyes begot it. This tongue bred it up.
> This breast would lodge it!

November 1874

(Beaumont & Fletcher, IX, 294) *The Maid in the Mill*

A perplexing foolish play with very little in it to interest the reader, however it may have suited the spectator. But I can hardly imagine that the plot of Antonio & Martine, of Ismenia & Aminta could have been intelligible even on the stage. Florimel could be pretty, but that there is so much nastiness in her assumed evil condition. The imitation of Shakespeare's low comic wit is very bad, — bad in amounting to mean plagiarism and bad also in its absolute want of humour. 24 November 1874

51

(Beaumont & Fletcher, IX, 387) *A Wife for a Month*

The point on which the interest of this play turns is to us, at this day, so unpalatable and gross, and must even in Fletcher's time have been chosen with so mere a desire to suit the lewdness of certain classes of men, that one cannot call this a good play, but yet the execution is wonderful and the language often magnificent

> Oh misery.
> Had I seen my Valerio, know Evanthe
> I would have been with thee under a gallows
> Though the hangman had been my Hymea and the Furies
> Had some whips and forks ready to torture me —

This is very taking. 15 June 1874

(Beaumont & Fletcher, IX, 477) *Rule a Wife and Have a Wife*

This must have been an excellent play for acting when it was possible to put on the stage so disgusting a character as that of Margarita. Leon was I believe a favourite character with both Garrick and Kemble, and I think the play was specially re-arranged for Kemble. But, as is the case with most of Fletcher's plays the motives of the persons are so bad as to rob the piece of all sympathy. And the changes in the disposition of the personages are so unnatural as to make the reader feel that the author regarded simply the stage effects, and not any subsequent appreciation of his work by a reading public. 1 July 1870

(Beaumont & Fletcher, X, 105) *The Fair Maid of the Inn*

A very sorry performance surely. No sympathy can be felt for any of the higher characters. There is but little poetry in the language. Since Bianca the heroine does not move us and the comedy of Forobosco and the clown is as poor as anything from Fletcher's hand. Like so much of Fletchers work the whole play was written at a gallop. One passage of Bianca may be excepted from this criticism, but even that is nothing excessive

> Thus to yield up, then,
> The cottage of my virtue, to be swallow'd
> By some hard neighboring landlord, such as you are,
> Is in effect to love? A lord so vicious?
> Oh, where shall Innocence find some poor dwelling
> Free from Temptation's tyranny?

The character of Cesario is absolutely disgusting; — and it is disgusting that she should have married him at last. 18 September 1874

(Beaumont & Fletcher, X, 195) *The Noble Gentleman*

Excellent fooling from beginning to end. I know nothing of the kind better. 15 June 1874

(Beaumont & Fletcher, X, 292) *The Elder Brother*

I cannot quite give my sanction to all that Dyce says about this play; — but, without a doubt, the character of Charles contains very fine pieces of poetry. Nearly all that is good is put into his mouth, — but some of it is very good for instance.

> We'll lose ourselves in Venus' groves of myrtle,
> Where every little bird shall be a cupid,
> And sing of love and youth; each wind that blows,
> And curls the velvet leaves, shall breed delights;
> The wanton springs shall call us to their banks,
> And on the perfumed flowers we'll feast our senses;

I cannot say that the reform of Eustace, the younger brother, is very happy. 3 July 1874

(Beaumont & Fletcher, X, 369) *The Nice Valour*

Taken as an entire play this piece is absurd beyond expression. It is hard to conceive how any playwright could have made so confused and purposeless a plot. But there are one or two redeeming passages. Act II sc i Chamont

> And, since it is not in the power of monarchs
> To make a gentleman, which is a substance
> Only begot of merit, they should be careful
> Not to destroy the worth of one so rare,
> Which neither they can make, nor, lost, repair.

and again act III scene ii Duke's sister.

> He loved for goodness, not for wealth or lust,
> After the world's foul dotage; he never courted
> The body, but the beauty of the mind,
> A thing which common courtship never thinks on.

29 September 1874

(Beaumont & Fletcher, X, 467-68) *The Bloody Brother, or Rollo, Duke of Normandy*

This is unlike most of Fletcher's plays in having the finer passages in the latter acts. The two first acts having nothing to recommend them and are laden with the stiffest and most turgid rhymes. The conduct of the plot is horrible, and the characters are either simply detestable, or else as weak as water. That of Aubrey is so, and also of Edith.

There are, however, — as in almost all these plays, — some isolated gems worth the seeking, as

> Princes may pick their suffering nobles out,
> And one by one employ them to the block;
> But when they once grow formidable to
> Their clowns and cobblers; — 'ware then; [sic, !]
>   guard themselves!

Edith's curse, Act III scene i, — too long to quote here, — was surely running in Byron's head when he put his curse into the mouth of Marino Faliero. The "When" runs through them both.

Fletcher's songs are for the most part worthless; but in this play there is one that has always been loved.

> "Take, oh, take those lips away."

October 1874

(Beaumont & Fletcher, XI, 118) *The Lovers' Progress*

The writing in this more careful than with Fletcher generally; — some very fine passages, — especially in the night scene between Calista and Lysander, — but then rendering [?] the plot outrageous, and the characters all untrue to nature. 10 October 1874

(Beaumont & Fletcher, XI, 213) *The Night-Walker or The Little Thief*

This play must I think be altogether unsatisfactory to readers of this age; and yet I can understand that it should have been a very good acting play in the days of James I. It is full of action and coarse fun, and points to be made by high mettled actors. It has no pathos, and no human nature. Every person in the action is false, fraudulent and mischievous, and yet they all turn out good at last. It seems to me to be very unlike Fletcher, who seldom dealt with English characters. I should think it to be chiefly the work of Shirley who laid his scene in England much oftener than did Fletcher. 25 December 1874

(Beaumont & Fletcher, XI, 323) *Love's Pilgrimage*

A lively play, but very confused — It has some passages nearly fine, but nothing quite worthy of special remark. Fletcher's great fault of pardoning all sin for the sake of final effect is displayed most grossly in the character of Marc Antonio. Nothing can be viler than this man, and yet at the end he comes out as the happy lover and thriving gentleman. But Fletcher had no wish of carrying with him the sympathies of his audience as to character. The closeness with which Fletcher copied the plots from which he drew his material is manifested in this play; and also his tendency to crib from Shakespeare. 27 December 1874

(Beaumont & Fletcher, XI, 437-39) *The Two Noble Kinsmen*

There is no play in the English language more open to conjecture as to its authorship than this, or as to which the question is more interesting. Taken as a whole it is the finest piece of poetry printed among the works of Beaumont & Fletcher. Three names are mentioned, those of Fletcher, Chapman and Shakespeare. That the play contains work of Shakespeare and Fletcher is undoubted. The evidence as to Chapman is very loose. Shakespeare is generally thought to have written the first and fifth acts. To me his work is much plainer in the first than the fifth; — but even in the first there is something that is not his. He is, however, to be found in the other three, — certainly in the second and third. In the fifth his hand has been much overlaced by the coarser work of Fletcher. There are passages in the play very much finer than are to be found in some of Shakespeare's unquestioned work. The well known lines in the First Queen's speech. Act I sc. i

> "When her arms,
> "Able to lock Jove from a synod &c

Nobody but Shakespeare could have written. In Act II scen. i

> No, Palamon,
> Those hopes are prisoners with us

and

> She locks her beauties in her bud again

and act III sc i

> Oh, Queen Emilia,
> Fresher than May, sweeter
> Than her gold buttons on the boughs, or all
> Th' enamelled knacks of the mead or garden! yea
> We challenge too the bank of any nymph,
> That makes the stream seem flowers;

Surely these passages are Shakespeare all over, — though he is generally held to have had but little to do with Acts II & III. 8 October 1874

[This play is marked liberally in pencil throughout. Some of Trollope's notes include the following:

Beside Arcite's lines (I.iii) "Let him approach:/ But that we fear the gods in him," Trollope writes "can not be Shakespeare". At the end of Act I (p. 352), Trollope writes "very much in this act much too obscure for Shakespeare"

Beginning Act II, beside the jailer's first speech, Trollope writes: "Surely Shakespeare wrote this"

Beside the lines quoted above in his own note from Act II.i, "No, Palamon" Trollope writes: "Shakespeare all over"

In the same scene, beside the long exchange between Arcite and Palamon, Trollope draws a long line (actually beginning beside the line "Let's think the prison holy sanctuary") and writes: "Surely Fletcher never wrote anything so simply worded as is this—"

At the end of Act IV. i, Trollope writes: "The whole of this scene is wonderfully well copied from Shakespeare, — written as though Fletcher wished to have it thought to be Shakespeare's."]

Child, Francis James, ed. *Four Old Plays.* Cambridge: George Nichols, 1848.

(Child, I, 89) *The Pardoner and the Frere* [John Heywood]

It is excellent good comedy, full of good broad honest fun, without vulgarity, fit to be read by all, and wonderfully suggestive as to those cuts [?] which both Luther and the Reformation strove to heal. Heywood was a staunch Romanist, and, such being the case, his evidence is the more valuable. The abominations of the Pardoner, who is twice worse than the Frere are admirably described. The language is very different from that which grew into use but a short time afterwards, — but to John Heywood probably affected the use of old words and old spelling. October 1873

(Child, I, 260) *Jocasta* [Gascoigne & Kenwelmershe]

This is long and dull, with the old-fashioned sententiousness of the Greek play without its terseness; but the versification is sonorous and very perfect. It has of course the monotonous cadence which was manifestly pleasing to English ears till it was broken up by the more composite melody of Shakespeare and others. This is interesting as the second English play we have in blank verse and the first adaptation of a play from the Greek. 28 October 1873

Dekker, Thomas. *The Dramatic Works*. 6 vols. London: John Pearson, 1873.

[In the Memoir (p. xxxvii) at the beginning of the plays, Pearson quotes Charles Lamb's "praise" of Dekker's part in writing one of the plays: "This scene has beauties of so very high an order that, with all my respect for Massinger, I do not think he had poetical enthusiasm capable of finishing them." Trollope writes in the margin: "There is nothing more gloriously absurd in criticism than the decisive statements made by the friends of Massinger and the friends of Dekker!"]

(Dekker, I, 79) *The Gentle Craft*

There is a good rattle of quaint fun in this piece, though not very much wit. It is praised with much too loud a mouth in the preface, — as is natural. An editor always thinks the piece he is handling to be the best of its kind. We are told of the love story which runs through the play like a silver thread. Now we are certainly told very often of the love of Lacy & Rose, — and the two run away and are married, — but there is no story of love such as Shakespeare tells, or Ford occasionally, or Fletcher. The story goes no further than to let us know that a young nobleman neglects his duty in order that he may marry a girl beneath him. 22 November 1873

(Dekker, I, 174) *Comedie of Olde Fortunatus* [compare (Di, III, 219)]

The story of the various wishes and the folly of the wish for wealth has come to us in many shapes, — but in none more tedious than this. Yet there is such a richness of language in the play that it is worth reading. The childishness of all the persons, and the simple superlativeness of vice and virtue did not strike an audience temp: Eliz: as it does us. 23 November 1873

(Dekker, I, 264) *The Untrussing of the Humorous Poet*

This play is full of wit, and a most excellent answer to Jonsons Poetaster; — but read in conjunction with the Poetaster declares too plainly the inferiority of Dekker to Jonson. One is sorry that it should be so, as one feels that Jonson should not have attacked Dekker and the other play-wrights; and that Dekker behaved with spirit in answering him.

It is said in the notes that Crispinis was meant for Marston, and Fannius for Dekker. This must be wrong. Crispinis was Dekker, — as may be seen by the allusion to Dekkers head of hair in the Poetaster.

The would-be semi-tragedy of the poisoning of the bride who was to have been given up to the king is absurd. If tragedy and comedy are combined in one piece, the tragedy should never have to give way to the comedy, — as it does here. Nevertheless there are a few fine lines. 16 November 1873

(Dekker, I, 326) *The King's Entertainment Through the City of London*
A thing impossible to read —

(Dekker, II, 91) *The Honest Whore* [(cr. Do, III, 322); (cr. Mi, III, 122)]
In this play there are three stories; first that of the deaths of the Duke's daughter and of the Duke's daughter's lover, — both fictitious. This is not well told and is uninteresting. Then there is the tale of the longing wife; — which is absurd but so told as to amuse. Thirdly there is the story of the whore, — who is herself by no means very honest, at last. Having been converted from her prostitution by sudden love for one man, she is happy to settle down in life in an enforced marriage with another. But this story is graced by so strong a denunciation of prostitution from the lips of the man whom the whore loves as to make the whole thing remarkable for its force. I know no play of the time in which there is a more continued flavour stolen from Shakespeare. November 1873

(Dekker, II, 183) *The Honest Whore, Part II* [(cr. Do, III, 425); (cr. Mi, III, 244)]
This is a poorer play than the last, — very coarse, and very confused. There is, however, a life about it, which I can understand should have recommended it to the lovers of theatre of the time.

This edition is very poor. It is a simple reprint of an early edition, with all its blunders. A list of the persona of the play has not even been added. The editor would say that such was not the purpose. But why not? 6 December 1873

(Dekker, III, 232) *The Roaring Girle or Moll Cut-Purse* [see (Mi, II, 559); (Do, VI, 106)]
See Middleton's works vol. 2 and Dodsley's Plays vol. 6

(Dekker, IV, 91) *The Virgin Martir* [see (Mas, I, 121)]
See Massinger's works.

58

(Dekker, IV, 286) *The Wonder of a Kingdome* [verbatim (Di, III, 98)]

This is a most ridiculous play, made up as it were of the leavings of other plays, — half a dozen scraps of plots, so brought together that nothing should be lost; the very omnium-gatherum of an overdone playwright. 11 April 1880

(Dekker, IV, 344) *The Sun's Darling* [see (F, III, 169)]

See Fords works Jan 75

(Dekker, IV, 427) *The Witch of Edmonton* [see (F, III, 271)]

See Fords works Jan. 1875

Dilke, Charles Wentworth, ed. *Old Plays; Being a Continuation of Dodsley's Collection.* 6 vols. London: Rodwell and Martin, 1816.

(Dilke, I, 88) *The Tragedy of Doctor Faustus* [Marlowe; compare (Mar, II, 84)]

The fine passages in this play are few and very short. The speech to Helen's ghost is his finest. The quick falling down from poetic height to grovelling language is such as to leave a final subject [?] very much against the work. Marlowe never creates sympathy. With his Faustus no one really cares whether the Devil has him or no. 2 December 1867

(Dilke, I, 195) *Lust's Dominion* [Marlowe]

A most absurd play, out-Heroding all absurdity in it's [sic] confusion, — shewing the taste of the age for unlimited villainy, but confining itself to no possibility of action. Now and again it nearly touches the realm of poetry, but never quite reaches it. One can understand that Marlowe should have been accredited with its bombast, — though the doing so has done an injury to Marlowe's memory. 20 October 1879

(Dilke, I, 287) *Mother Bombie* [Lyly]

This [sic] an exceedingly silly play arranged after the fashion of the comedies of Terence, — as was Shakespeare's Comedy of Errors. The dialogue is utterly wanting in wit, and the plot is beyond measure tedious. I cannot imagine why any editor should have reprinted so bad a piece. 23 July 1870

(Dilke, I, 371) *Midas: A Comedy* [Lyly]

Nothing could be less fit for the stage than the cumbersome nature of Lyly's language; a worse play than Midas could hardly be produced. 20 October 1879

(Dilke, II, 97) *Endymion: or the Man in the Moon* [Lyly]

There is a certain prettiness as well as quaintness, — a poetry and also an affectation, — in the speeches of Endymion, Cynthia and Eumenides which makes the play readable. The parts that are intended to be funny, Sir Tophas and the Pages, are below criticism. 16 November 1879

(Dilke,II,191) *History of Antonio and Mellida* [Marston; compare (Mars, I, 68-9)]

Read Jan 9 71 See Marston's works

It is almost inconceivable that so bad a play should have lived so long and enjoyed a reputation. It is bad in plot language and character. The plot is almost meaningless. Now and again a line occurs which is worth preserving; — as for instance

> As having clutched a rose
> Within my palm, the rose being taken away
> My hand retains a little breath of scent [sic, sweet].

9 January 1871

(Dilke, II, 290) *What You Will* [Marston; compare (Mars, I, 218)]

What You Will is a good comedy, with some fine lines; with much humour but terribly confused; loaded with unnecessary characters and often unintelligible in its language. That which is intended to be sarcasm on the bombast of other writers is itself so bombastic as to lose the flavour of wit. October 1867

(Dilke, II, 407) *Parasitaster; or The Fawn* [Marston; compare (Mars, II, 106)]

There is much wit and a little, — but only a very little, — poetry in the play. It seems to have been left by the author in great confusion of language, which has been made worse by the Editor who has retained all his spellings as though there were some hidden purpose in them. In all our Tudor and Stuart plays one regrets Dyce when Dyce is is [sic] absent.

There is some fooling on the word "only" in this play of which I do not see the purpose. 15 November 1879

60

(Dilke, III, 98) *The Wonder of a Kingdom* [Dekker; verbatim (De, IV, 286)]

This is a most ridiculous play, made up as it were of the leavings of other plays, — half a dozen scraps of plots so brought together that nothing should be lost; the very omnium-gatherum of an overdone playwright. 11 April 1880

(Dilke, III, 219) *Old Fortunatus* [Dekker; compare (De, I, 174)]

The story of the various wishes and the folly of the wish for wealth has come to us in many shapes; — but in none more tedious than in this. Yet there is such a richness of language in the play that it is worth reading. The childishness of all the passions and the simple superlativeness of vice and virtue did not strike an audience, — temp Eliz, — as it does us. 23 Nov. 1873

(Dilke, III, 341) *Bussy D'Ambois* [Chapman]

There are passages of exquisite poetry in this most unintelligible of plays. The character of D'Ambois, brave, all-subduing, arrogant, and untameable is very fine. Of his love for the married lady & the assistance of the friar it is hard to understand anything. It seems to be presumed that the love though adulterous should be regarded as innocent. The marvel is, — how could an audience of that day should have followed [sic] such a play on the stage. 10 November 1879

(Dilke, III, 433) *Monsieur D'Olive: A Comedy* [Chapman]

This is a thoroughly bad play, — very little worthy of being included in this collection. The author has not taken the trouble so to arrange his ideas as to make plain his plots. He seems to have had two, the one of some foolish ambassador, and the other altogether unintelligible of the two ladies. But who is husband to whom, or the reverse, no one can tell. 1 April 1880

(Dilke, IV, 114) *May Day: A Comedy* [Chapman]

There is some drollery in this piece, and a certain pleasantness in the willingness of Emilia to be wooed and her bashfulness under the operation; — but the play throughout is confused, and this work like that of Chapman generally, is far too hurried to be worthy of praise. 21 February 1880

61

(Dilke, IV, 218) *The Spanish Gipsy* [Middleton and Rowley; see (Mi, IV, 202)]

This play is often tedious and sometimes obscure, but there is much in it good in action and something of real poetry. Ap. 1878

(Dilke, IV, 323) *The Changeling : A Tragedy* [Middleton and Rowley; compare (Mi, IV, 300)]

There is much movement in this play and there are scenes of interest. But it is so confused and inconsequent that the reader can too readily perceive the quick unnatural way in which the dramatists of Jas. I worked at the plots which fell in their way. There is, however, more good work in this play than ever elsewhere came from Middleton's hands. 20 April 1878

(Dilke, IV, 428-29) *More Dissemblers Besides Women* [Middleton; compare (Mi, III, 645)]

This play like most of Middleton's is hard reading. I can understand that there should have been amusement from the acting. According to the humour of the time there would have been fun in the singing master and dancing master giving lessons to the poor mock page when she was about to fall into the straw. And in the dignity of the Duchess and the hypocrisy of the Cardinal there may have been amusement. All the various underplots no doubt served, though each severally is poor. But as a play for the closet there is nothing in it. 27 April 1877

(Dilke, V, 127) *Women Beware Women* [Middleton; compare (Mi, IV, 635)]

See Middleton's works October 8 1876
The execution of the 3 first acts of this play is so good as to make the critic feel that Middleton, had he given himself fair chance by continued labour might have excelled all the Elizabethan dramatists except Shakespeare. But the plot is so detestable that the same critic is driven to acknowledge that with all his power of language the author could never have become a great poet. That Brancha and Livia should have been abominable one would have endured, had not Isabella been as bad. Her conscience was so made easy when she was brought to think that her paramour was not Guardiano her uncle. The execution of the last part of the play is as bad as the plot. But it has to be acknowledged that there is wonderful work in the three first acts. 8 October 1876

(Dilke, V, 224) *A Trick to Catch the Old One* [Middleton; verbatim (Mi, II, 99)]

See Middleton's works 15 January 1877
I cannot call this a good play, though I can understand that it should have been lively on the stage. The fun is all low in its nature, and of poetry there is little or none. As to the morality the less said the better. 15 January 1877

(Dilke, V, 348) *A New Wonder: A Woman Never Vext* [Rowley]

This is a fairly good play, easily to be understood, with an intelligible plot, but no poetry, above a line or two here and there. I found it readable and can conceive that it should be well-acted. 12 November 1879

(Dilke, V, 450) *Appius and Virginia: A Tragedy* [Webster]

This is a good tragedy, well devised and lucidly told, — readable throughout, — but it seldom rises to any grandeur of poetry— 23 November 1879

(Dilke, VI, 98) *The Thracian Wonder* [Webster and Rowley]

Dyce in rejecting this from Webster's works calls it a worthless drama. It is wonderfully confused and unmeaning in its plot; but it has some pretty poetry, and I can understand that it should have been a stirring play on the stage. 18 December 1878

(Dilke, VI, 218) *The English Traveller* [Th. Heywood; compare (H, IV, 95)]

This is a good play, — but much marred by the hurry with which the playwrights of this time went through their work. There is pathos in it, and poetry and an excellent though ill managed plot. 8 February 1880

(Dilke, VI, 321) *Royal King and Loyal Subject* [Th. Heywood; compare (H, VI, 83)]

There is an absence of life in this play which makes it cold throughout although the plot has been elaborated. The king, with whom we never sympathise, is put above everything so as to be inhuman. The husband is like Griselda, too good; and the captain, who never comes with [?] the marshall, is no more than a dummy. 16 March 1880

(Dilke, VI, 424) *A Challenge for Beauty* [Th. Heywood; virt. id. in (H, V, 78)]

The plot, or two plots, of this play are irregular and impossible, but there is some fine poetry and the reader feels that he has something to satisfy him. This is generally the case with Thomas Heywood when he works in a hurry. He composes a fine bit here and there but cannot give himself time to finish his play. Indeed he hardly cares to do so, so long as he may get paid

> "No nation, sex, complexion, birth degree
> "But jest at want and mock at misery"

and

> "Unkind man, — thou hast killed me!"

All this is fine. But Isabella and her husband are absurd. 19 April 1880

Dodsley, Robert, ed. *A Collection of the Old English Plays.* 12 vols. London, 1825-27.

(Dodsley, I, clxix) *Historia Histrionica* [Wright]

Hardly worth perusal, except as confirming the statements made in Dodsley's Preface.*

[*Dodsley (p. cxli) says: "Old plays will be always read by the curious, if it were only to discover the manners and behaviour of several ages and how they altered. For plays are exactly like portraits, drawn in the garb and fashion of the time when painted."]

(Dodsley, I, 42) *God's Promises* [Bale]

To me all the work of the time of Henry VIII is very pleasing, having a simple earnestness and a graphic unaffected euphony which were very often missed by the great men of the following reigns. The argument and conduct of this poem of Bale's are very interesting, and well worth perusing, and there is a poetry about it altogether without pretense. March 1874

(Dodsley, I, 102) *The Four P's* [John Heywood]

This is full of wit, and strongly relishes of the old English fun which flavours all the plays we have of the time of Henry VIII. But I think it hardly equal to the Pardoner and the Frere (by the same author). And this piece is subject to censure on the score of obscenity, — a fault not uncommon with the plays of that age. See how free from such dirt is Ralph Roister Doister. 24 October 1873

The two lies of the Poticary and the Pardoner are perhaps the best parts of this piece, — though the shorter lie of the Palmer takes the reward —

(Dodsley, I, 173) *Ferrex and Porrex* [Sackville & Norton]

Gorboduc or Ferrex and Porrex — I have not read the whole of this old play. It is tedious, and very deficient in dramatic action. The diction is certainly singularly poetical, and more than ordinarily equable, never falling into bathos or rising to sublimity, — never grandly nervous or absurdly weak. It could not now be endured upon the stage, whereas the comedy of Roister Doister,* *which is the only earlier English play we have*, would with slight alterations draw full houses. 11 July 1870

* This is not true. We can hardly say what is or what is not a play. Halliwell calls this the first regular historical play in the English language. It was the first play in blank verse.

(Dodsley, I, 260) *Damon and Pithias* [Edwards]

Neither in rhythm or in wit is this equal to other pre-Shakespearean plays. It can not on either ground approach Ralph Roister Doister which we may presume to be 30 years earlier, nor does it come near John Heywood's plays, which presumably were 20 years older than this. And yet for language it is as far-removed from the present day as either of them, and approaches as little to the language of Shakespeare — or of Marlowe.

The play is very much worth reading and has much of the homely raciness of the period of Henry VIII, which was driven away by the big mouths of the Elizabethan dramatists.

I doubt whether I know any other play without a female character. April 1874

(Dodsley, I, 307-08), *New Custome* [anonymous]

The language of all these old pre-dramatic plays, — whether in the shape of moralities such as this, or on the rare of early [?] English life is pleasing healthy strong and thoroughly honest. Nor is there anything to disgust. The argument here in favour of protestantism as against papacy is not very strong; but there is much good hearty abuse, accompanied with sound assurance. And though the reader may doubt the speedy conversion of 'Perverse Doctrine', still he can understand that such pieces would be and no doubt were an assistance to the Reformation. The passage touching on clerical vestments is very good.

But he who puts his religion in wearing the thing,
Or thinks himself more holy for the contrary doing,
Shall prove but a fool, of whatever condition
He be, for sure, that is but mere superstition.

6 October 1878

[Trollope has modernized the spelling in the quotation.]

(Dodsley, II, 83) *Gammer Gurton's Needle* [Still?; (cr. Ha, I, 242)]

The chief marvel of this old comedy is that so much room for wit should have been found in dealing with so trivial a subject. The broad good-humoured [sic] fun of the piece cannot be denied, nor a certain apt flow in the metre which pleases the ear. The play is very dirty, or perhaps what we should better call vulgar — rustical as such jocularity used to be termed — "Country matters". No doubt the word rustical was correct. The dirty jokes of Gammer Gurton and her friends and foes was probably common in country in plays in the early days of Elizabeth, but had already been banished from the cities. It is remarkable that in Ralph Roister Doister, — the scene of which is laid in London, but which was probably written 30 years before Gammer Gurton's needle [sic], — there is little or nothing of this foul language.

In these two comedies, the plot, though very different, is conducted on the same lines. A merry mischievous varlet sets every one at sixes and sevens, makes the women fight, causes skulls to be cracked, and gets off himself with cakes and ales.

Gammer Gurton's Needle, by a reformed clergyman, deals very hardly with the Church in the person of Vicar Rat; whereas Ralph Roister Doister, the product of a papal period, makes no ill allusion to the church.

The oath administered by the Bayly [sic, Bailye] to Diccon is no doubt the forerunner of the Highgate oath,* which I myself took when I was young, and was probably an old established joke when the comedy was written. 16 July 1870

[* "In the time of stage coaches a custom was introduced of making ignorant persons" swear to an oath before they were allowed the "freedom of the Highgate." The fine of admission, discussed after the oath was taken, was a bottle of wine. "Highgate." *Encyclopaedia Britannica.* Vol. 11. 9th ed. 1880.]

(Dodsley, II, 150) *Alexander and Campaspe* [Lyly]

The two songs in the play are the best of it. It is readable, — which is more than can be said of the author's novel. But there is but little in it, except quaint language. The wit of Diogenes and the servants is but would-be wit, poor and far fetched. As for the lovers, their love is all words, and they are as cold in their love as fishes. 17 July 1870

(Dodsley, II, 234) *Tancred and Gismunda* [Wilmot]

In this, Tancred and Gismunda, as in most of the pre-Shakespearean tragedies the reader has to reach far for few pearls. There is a certain sustained grandeur of language, — often however closely bordering on the absurd, and rarely devoted to the delineation of natural characters. The following lines are so pretty that they might well be set to music

> Wert thou not mine, dear heart, whil'st that my love
> Danced and played upon thy golden strings?
> Art thou not mine, dear heart, now that my love
> Is fled to heaven, and got him golden wings?

1 January 1871
Truth compels me to acknowledge that I have skipped the choruses.

(Dodsley, II, 303) *Cornelia* [Kyd]

Perhaps the fact that a man should have written so long a poem so utterly devoid of interest is not so singular as that an Editor should have found it worth his while to reproduce it! Why did Dodsley put it into his collection? Did any man ever read it? For it is simply unreadable. 13 October 1878

(Dodsley, II, 404) *Edward II* [Marlowe; see (Mar, II, 290)]

See Marlowe's works. Read Dec. 1, 1867

(Dodsley, III, 48) *George a Greene, the Pinner of Wakefield* [Greene?; compare (G, II, 205)]

There is much life and movement in George a Greene; but it by no means equals R. Roister Doister in nature or language, nor Gammer Gurton's needle [sic] in wit. It is free from the vulgarity of the latter. 2 Jan. 1870

[Trollope marks with an X an early passage in the play (p. 17) when James threatens Jane:

> Then list to me, saint Andrew be my boot,
> But I'll rase thy castle to the very ground,
> Unless thou open the gate, and let me in.

At the bottom of the page Trollope pencils in these lines:
> Come down, come down, Lady Ogilvie. Oh
> Come down and kiss me fairly.

67

Or I swear by the sword that hangs at my side
I'll not leave a stanning stone in Airlie.
(standing) [sic]   ]

(Dodsley, III, 94) *Jeronimo* [Kyd?]

Abominable trash. This play has had a name; but it has come I take it, as did that of the succeeding piece, simply from its absurdity. 2 January 1871

We are told that Ben Jonson ranked Kyd with Lyly & Marlowe. How could he rank any writer with two others so dissimilar and unequal? No two writers were ever more unlike than Lyly and Marlowe — of whom the former was simply quaint in language (see his Alexander and Campaspe) and the other was vehemently forcible in language and in plot also.

(Dodsley, III, 202) *Spanish Tragedy* [Kyd]

For tediousness, improbability, and turgid pomposity this play is probably unequalled, but in its day it was popular, and there is that in the grief of the father which is not without a certain effect of pathos. 2 January 1871

[On p. 54, beside the opening lines of Act IV, Trollope says: "writ probably before Macbeth"]

(Dodsley, III, 322) *The Honest Whore* [Dekker; see (De, II, 91); (cr. Mi, III, 122)]

See Dekker's works.

(Dodsley, III, 425) *The Honest Whore, Part II* [Dekker; see (De, II, 183); (cr. Mi, III, 244)]

See Dekker's works.

(Dodsley, IV, 96) *The Malcontent* [Marston; see (Mars, II, 292)]

Read on January 1871. See Marston's works.

(Dodsley, IV, 182) *All Fools* [Chapman]

This play as far as the plot is concerned might have been written by Terence. The two old men and their sons, and the sons' mistresses are Terentian all through. The play is very uneven, — the first act admirably conceived and written. Then it falls off, — though with many excellent pieces. Sometimes especially in act IV it is very poor. The second plot about Cornelio is poor. The women are naught in the action or diction. 14 June 1873

(Dodsley, IV, 279) *Eastward Hoe* [Jonson; compare (Mars, III, 101-2)]

This is a most tedious play, with very little humour, and altogether unworthy of Ben Jonson's name. This is the story (which was probably current long before,) of the diligent and idle apprentice; but even the moral is travestied, as at the end, the joke consists in the old tradesman being taken in by the mock repentance of the idle one.

What a job it must have been, what a cutting of blocks with razors, to edit such stuff as this with care, comparing various editions, line by line. 7 June 1873

It should be remembered that to the audience much of the delight of many plays of the time, — and apparently of this one, — arose from satyre of things of the day which we only partially understand. Quicksilver's "Repentance" was of this nature, and is thus partially justified, tho' it destroys all the moral of the play.

(Dodsley, IV, 370) *The Revenger's Tragedy* [Tourneur?]

This is one of those tortured plays with extravagant half digested plots and violent language, — often unintelligible, — which the reign of James I produced. It nearly rises to fine poetry in many of the scenes, but never quite does so in any part. Nor is any one character satisfactory; — that of Vindice on which the plot hangs coming nearest to the mark. The play is certainly worth reading. 10 May 1874

(Dodsley, IV, 451-52) *The Dumb Knight* [Machin and Markham]

We are told that this play is from the hands of two persons, Lewis Machin and Gervase Markham. Not only have there been, very manifestly two authors, — but also two stories, two plots, and two different modes of story telling.

The Dumb Knight ceases to be dumb in the middle of the third act, and after that there is no reference to his dumbness, — or to the reward which he takes for his persistency, or to that which the Lady ought to enjoy. Everything is changed, and we come to the unreasonable villainy of the Duke of Epire. The reader cannot but feel that in the first half of the play there is a fairly good plot, with very *much most sweet poetry.* One is led to hope that the play is going to be a play indeed. But the second half is, in plot and versification, as bad as the first is good. Why does the Duke of Epire wish to destroy the king? and the king's wife? and Philocles? And why does the king listen to him?

This, however is clear, — that between between [sic] the two authors there was no mutual plot. Two writers, each unable to make out five acts, have combined two stories, — with unequal powers, — one being a poet and the other merely a fabricator of verses.

The indecent part of both is, as is usual, bad and disgusting. 18 June 1876

[p. 446, toward the end of the play, Trollope says this about the battle: "Surely the fight in Ivanhoe was taken from this."]

(Dodsley, V, 97) *Inforced Marriage* [Wilkins] [a penciled comment, now unreadable, has been written over in ink]

This is so infamously bad that one can hardly understand how it should have come to be printed in this fashion, or that such a play should have been annotated in this way by a learned man! It has no taste or sign of so early a date as that given to it; and is, as we see it here, probably the work of Mrs. Aphra Behn. [No date]

(Dodsley, V, 214) *Lingua* [Brewer?]

This comedy is replete with wit and erudition. In spite of the absurdity of its elements, (which bring it rather within the lines of a burlesque than a comedy,) it contains many passages of fine poetry; — and some pieces of poetry and broad fun combined such as are seen in the old dramatists and hardly to be found elsewhere — as when Mendacio says Act II scene vi

> When I beheld hot Mars and Mercury
> With rackets made of spheres and balls of stars
> Playing at tennis for a tun of Nectar.

21 June 1873

[Near the end of Act I.vii., p. 118, Trollope marks the speeches by Olfactus and Tactus and says: "Shewing that these plays were written first in prose and then turned into verse — for which latter work the endurance of the author was sometimes insufficient."]

(Dodsley, V, 272) *The Merry Devil* [anonymous]

A good rattling comedy with some fun in it for a good-humoured [sic] audience, — but hardly worth the reading. I cannot think much of the judgement of him who thought it to be Shakespeare's work. 14 December 1878

(Dodsley, V, 358) *A Mad World* [Middleton; see (Mi, II, 422)]

See Middleton's works 23 April 1878.

(Dodsley, V, 459-60) *Ram-Alley or Merry Tricks* [Barry]

This piece tho' vulgar and full of coarse ribaldry is excellent reading, and very superior to many plays of the period which was of all times the most prolific in plays. It was manifestly written during the first 7 or 8 years of James I. There is a thorough trace of Nym and Pistol and a most close resemblance to all the ways of life as described by Ben Jonson. But I doubt whether there be any play of Ben Jonson with a sprightlier wit. Then, however, as in almost any one of Jonsons plays, there is no room for sympathy. It was but rarely that any one of them, except Shakespeare, touched the heart. 16 October 1878

(Dodsley, VI, 106) *The Roaring Girl* [Middleton; compare (Mi, II, 559); (cr. De, III, 232)]

A most unintelligible gallemafrey [sic], — unreadable as a whole, and but little worth the labour of this attempt; but with sparkles of such wit as was then popular. It is undivided into acts, and therefore the more confused. This, and many plays of James I were probably written in great haste to satisfy the demand of the stage. They are hardly worth looking at, except giving pictures of the period. 7 August 1873

(Dodsley, VI, 202) *Widow's Tears* [Chapman]

The characters are disgusting, — as is also the second plot as to Cynthia, whereas the first plot as to Eudora is so weak as to be altogether without interest. But, nevertheless, the play is a good play, from the rapidity of the action and the force of the language. There are in it two different stories combined without any apparent link. 26 October 1878

(Dodsley, VI, 325-26) *The White Devil* [Webster]

Dyce speaks with very strong admiration of this play, saying that it is eminently interesting, and asking with enthusiasm how great must have been the genius which conceived so forcible and so consistent a character as Vittoria!! I cannot accede to this, and I think that Dyce so immersed himself in Elizabethan plays, that he became, (though the best of Editors,) at the same time the most laudatory of critics. No doubt there are strong passages in the play; but the whole is so confused as almost to make a key necessary for the interpretation of the incidents, and the character of Vittoria has to be guessed at throughout. She is not elucidated, nor do I think that it was clear in the author's own brain. The trial scene; of which Dyce speaks so strongly, contains no no [sic] trial.

71

Neither is guilt admitted by Vittoria nor proved against her. Her judge is simply her enemy, and for all that the reader knows she may be innocent as those. The play has all that violence of language which with the dramatists of James I was regarded as strength. April 1874

(Dodsley, VI, 393) *The Hog Hath Lost His Pearl* [Tailor]

This is as bad as anything I know among the old English drama. It is unredeemed by any poetry, any wit, or, I may say, by any fun. There are two plots which are wholly unconnected; — that giving the name to the play being the more slender of the two [?]. The other is peculiarly disgusting and offensive to our sympathies. A man's betrothed bride is ravished by his friend, — and the fault is readily pardoned, not only by the friend, but also by the lady! But the worst of the play is in the arrangement of the lines as verse without ever a spark of poetry. 27 October 1878

(Dodsley, VI, 486) *The Four Prentices* [Th. Heywood; see (H, II, 254)]

Read January 1875. See Heywood's work.

(Dodsley, VII, 99) *Green's Tu Quoque* [Cook]

A very good play, of infinite wit and with some small scraps of poetry. The less said about the morality the better. 6 July 1873

(Dodsley, VII, 212) *Albumazar* [Tomkis]

This is an excellent comedy, full of action and good broad fun, — more than equal to the Comedy of Errors, and equal in plot and life to Twelfth Night in life and plot [sic] (though of course inferior in characters and language[)]. It is singular how much more the contrivance of the play is to that of Shakespeare's, than the generality of the comedies of the period which are more akin to Ben Jonson, or Fletcher. 28 December 1878

(Dodsley, VII, 289) *A Woman Killed with Kindness* [Th. Heywood; see (H, II, 157)]

See Heywood's works. 31 October 1878

[There are many markings in this edition of the play. Trollope writes two "good's", two "very good's", and an "excellent", all by speeches of Frankford. In the list of characters at the beginning of the play (p. 225), we find Mrs. Frankford and Mrs. Anne and Trollope writes beside them "This is very poor editing. They are the same person."]

(Dodsley, VII, 376) *A Match at Midnight* [Rowley]

This is a most unintelligible piece. I have found it impossible to follow it. The audience it must be presumed understood something of it. That there should not have been some broad fun in the acting I can perceive. 6 April 1879

(Dodsley, VII, 456-57) *The True Trojans* [Fisher?]

Amidst a cloud of bombast composed in the very worst style of Euphuistic phraseology there are in this piece many lines of grand poetry, and some of infinite sweetness. There are too one or two allusions to things strictly English, — as to the swans of the Thames. "Where a full choir sings of white surpliced swans." Act IV Sc. iv. The ecstasies of Eulinus on the death of his mistress, are, though almost absurd in their inflation, still very near to grand poetry.

"Wither, ye pleasant gardens, where she trod"

& to Act IV Sc.v.

3 November 1878

(Dodsley, VIII, 10) *The Wounds of Civil War* [Lodge]

This is a remarkable play; — in the first place because of the continued excellence of the poetry which in some passages rises very high; and then on account of the bathos of silliness to which the comic portions sink, — as to which, however, it has to be owned that they are few and short.

The author has taken a period of Roman History very little known to ordinary readers, — and less one would think to an ordinary audience, — and made a tragedy out of a long period of time such as was in his time done by other dramatists out of the better known history of England. When one reads of Pompey, Antony, Lepidus and Octavius one hardly understands that one is being taken back to ante-Ciceronian times till one realizes Sylla and Marius. Who else has dramatised or even poetised Antony the orator? Who expects to meet a Lucretius prior to the poet, or a Scipio so insignificant that inscribed among the characters he should be introduced only once, and then not allowed to speak? The whole is taken from Plutarch and the characters both of Marius and Sylla are well conceived and well expressed.

Perhaps the greatest marvel is that men should have sat or rather stood, and listened to mere poetry with but little action, and no interest known or, probably, comprehensible to most of them. 22 December 1878

(Dodsley, VIII, 162) *The Heir* [May]

To my thinking a very poor play, though it is much praised by Halliwell.*
It is full of halting imitation from Shakespeare, in which the intended
pathos and intended drollery are equally lost. There are some good lines
in the 4th act. Otherwise the piece has been written with too much hurry
for poetry. No character has sufficient life or spirit to create sympathy. 19
January 1879

[*Halliwell (p. 115) says "The plot, language, and conduct of this play are all admirable, and
many of the situations interesting...."]

(Dodsley, VIII, 240) *Friar Bacon and Friar Bungay* [Greene; compare
(G, I, 214)]

The mixture of fine poetry and of absolute nonsense is very strange. The
marvel is that Shakespeare should have been so infinitely above his
contemporaries in arranging scenes and making language fit for after
ages. Greene was no doubt a scholar and a poet; but his works are now
caviare [sic] to the general. 4 January 1871

(Dodsley, VIII, 327) *The Jew of Malta* [Marlowe; see (Mar, I, 349)]

Read 24 November 1867. See Marlowe's works.

(Dodsley, VIII, 433) *The Wits* [Davenant]

The beginning of the play is droll enough, and is good reading; but it is
beyond measure long, and at last becomes tedious and unintelligible. I
can fancy that for the wants of the time it was a good acting comedy. 13
December 1878

(Dodsley, IX, 79) *Summer's Last Will* [*and Testament*] [Nash]

It is impossible to conceive any piece less worthy of being read than this.
There is nothing in it to interest, amuse, or even to occupy the mind.
How can any audience have listened to it even when the jokes were jokes
of the time? How can any editor have endured to edit it? Why should
Doddsley [sic] or any other collector have reprinted it?

The fate of some of these plays is very common. Here in this volume
are two of which hardly anyone now ever hears. There is this which is
unreadable, — and the Queen of Arragon, a play excellent with purpose,
nearly equal to Shakespeare. They are reprinted with equal honour and
apparently with equal chance of being read. 6 January 1879

(Dodsley, IX, 137) *Microcosmus* [Nabbes]

One cannot understand how it can have been that any audience should have listened to versification so tame. [No date, but recorded by Trollope in Halliwell (p. 170) as 16 October 1879.]

(Dodsley, IX, 225) *The Muse's Looking Glass* [Randolph]

This is very good reading, though any thing but dramatic. I cannot imagine such a work produced on the stage. But each separate part has its point well developed; and the lines are well written throughout, — with the exception of those referring to Philotimus & which are included to gratify the audience a little by indecency. They are very foul. The others are in this way, all good. 16 January 1880

(Dodsley, IX, 328) *The City-Match* [Mayne]

The plots here are too deep to be intelligible, but the play is full of life and is readable. 1 January 1880

(Dodsley, IX, 410) *The Queen of Arragon* [Habington]

I am disposed to say that there is finer poetry in this play than in any other drama in the English language beyond Shakespeare. And it is kept up throughout, — so thoroughly that even the comic character of Sanmartino is poetry throughout. Take the following lines act III sc. 1

> "The down on the swan's bosom,
> "Not white and soft as hers; — here! such a dew
> "As drops from bounteous heaven in the morning
> "To make the shadowy banks pregnant with violets"

& again — the same scene

> "The stars shoot
> "An equal influence on the open cottage,
> "Where the poor shepherds child is rudely nursed,
> "And on the cradle where the prince is rocked"

But it is nearly equal throughout — almost faultless in plot sentiment & language.

And yet no one has read it. None of those who are familiar with the names of Jonson Fletcher & Massinger have heard of Habington. His Castara is unknown. His play has crept in here, without a word of praise, by accident. 1 January 1879

[Trollope marks some passages in the play — the one quoted above in his comment, and Act II.i. p. 354 beside the banter of Browfildora and Captain ("Captain Cedar"), Trollope writes:

(Dodsley, X, 96) *The Antiquary* [Marmion]

A very good comedy, though marred by a ridiculously lame conclusion. In this, as in many comedies of the time, it seems to have been held sufficient to put bright language into the mouths of well drawn characters without much regard to the plot on hand.

Perhaps the best scene is that in which the so-called Bravo frightens Mocinigo by his mouthing buffoonery. 8 March 1874

(Dodsley, X, 161) *The Goblins* [Suckling]

This play is so confused that it is in many places unintelligible without more trouble in unravelling than it is worth. It has evidently been written in a great hurry for the stage, — so much so that the author has not given himself time for effect when effect would have been easy to him. Nevertheless, there are many sweet lines in it as would surely be the case in any thing written by Suckling. The character of Reginella might have been made very pretty had more trouble been taken with it. 11 January 1879

(Dodsley, X, 266) *The Ordinary* [Cartwright]

This is a most unintelligible piece, — not without wit in parts but so confused as to produce at this time no continuous lines of a plot. We must presume that when acted it did come home in some way to the minds of the audience. Allusions and customs were then recognised which are now altogether dark [?]. But I cannot conceive that it was ever thought a good play by those who had read Shakespeare. 15 March 1879

(Dodsley, X, 370) *A Jovial Crew* [Brome]

The four first acts are fairly good fun and I can understand that, for the time — they should have done well for the stage; — but he then falls off woefully in the fifth act. 10 February 1879

(Dodsley, X, 447) *The Old Couple* [May]

This is well worth reading, and is remarkable for its smooth versification. The sudden remorse and reform of the then avaricious old sinner is in the highest degree absurd; — but such sudden repentances were common in the plays of the day.

There is some allusion, twice made in the piece, to a chaplain wanting orders which I do not quite understand. 9 November 1878

(Dodsley, XI, 97) *Edward I* [Peele; compare (P, I, 200)]

This is a marvellous example of such a play as could give delight to the earlier part of Queen Elizabeths reign. It is an abridgement of the incidents of many years and is chiefly remarkable for the boldness with which the author could push on from one tortured [?] detail to another without a pause. There is not much poetry in it; — but there is some, and a somewhat grand idea of the feeling of a King and Queen. The historical ignorance of the author is shewn by the introduction of all the horror contained in the mythical ballad as to Q. Ellinor [sic]. No doubt the other incidents were taken from equally popular sources. 20 November 1878

(Dodsley, XI, 183) *The Mayor of Quinborough* [Middleton?; compare (Mi, I, 222)]

This play is very hard reading, but is interesting as shewing what a gallemafrey [sic] a plot was pleasing to the frequenters of theatres in the reign of James I. There is such a variety of incident that it can all be included in one piece only by the insertion of dumb shows between the acts and yet with that aid it must have been very long. I cannot but think that it must also have been very tedious.

Simon the mayor has but very little to do with the play, the connexion between him and the Vortiger plot being only by the thongs of leather the mayor cut. He seems to have been introduced simply that the horse play of the character and the clown might be introduced on the stage. The present name has grown on the play probably because his portion of the action best pleased the audience.

Middleton constantly cribs from Shakespeare, and always does it badly, — Perhaps of all the so called Elizabethan dramatists he was the worst. 3 June 1874

(Dodsley, XI, 258-59) *Grim, The Collier of Croydon* [J.T.]

This is an amusing gallimafrey [sic] of two distinct plots of which the one which gives the name to the play is by far the slightest, and is forced in to give a portion of broad comedy to the audience. The name, as in other pieces of the kind (notably Lord Dundreary of our time) was probably not originally selected by the author, but was added afterwards from the popularity of an actor in a special part.

I agree with the Editor that the play is older than 1600. There is much in the manners described, — specially as to marriage, that shews that it was so. That idea of marrying being virtually and not caring much whether the bedding or the wedding came first is old. But I do not think, as the editor does (see Note p. 249) that it was prior to Gammer Gurton's Needle. The versification is certainly subsequent, and almost as certainly the language. 1 December 1879

(Dodsley, XI, 345) *The City Night-Cap* [Davenport]

A very bad play, unintelligible, confused, and unnatural, — containing some few — but very few, — good passages. 19 May 1880

(Dodsley, XI, 585) *The Parson's Wedding* [Killegrew]

A most lengthy and unmeaning play. I cannot understand why it has been inserted in this collection as it has no beauty of language, and consists only of ribaldry in poor and unmeaning fancies [?]. It can only have been in the action that such a play was acceptable. It was acted originally only by women, — to men ashamed [?] by its obscene jokes. It has nothing else to recommend it. 22 May 1880

(Dodsley, XII, 117) *The Adventures of Five Hours* [Tuke]

I have read 4 acts of this play and the half of the 5th, but could not get to the end. The complications are of such a nature that it is impossible to understand them. Don Antonio and Don Octavio have no separate identities, nor have Porcia & Camilla. There is a certain skill in the language which sometimes pleases, but the whole thing is very tedious. That an audience could have sat it out is amazing.

The character of Alva as given by a court poet of the time of Charles II is the most interest [sic] passage in the play. July 1873
And yet the play was at the time very highly thought of —

(Dodsley, XII, 212) *Elvira* [Digby]

I have read the three first acts of this play and find it impossible to read the remainder. The plot is so involved that I never know who is who — that I cannot remember which man is intriguing with which woman; and the language is so unpoetical and indifferent, that no justification is to be found in its manner. The syllables in each line have been shown correctly counted; — and in that the poetry consists. 11 May 1880

(Dodsley, XII, 295) *The Widow* [Beaumont & Fletcher; see (BF, IV, 383); (cr. Mi, III, 440)]

See Beaumont & Fletcher. November 1874 In spite of Dyce's eulogy (see his edition,) I must declare this to be a poor play. A part, but only a small part in Act V is, I should say by Fletcher. The 4th act, which is said to be by Jonson, seems to be hardly better than the others. This is a grotesqueness in forcing dialogue so absolutely English into the mouths of Italians and laying the scene at Capo d'Istria. 30 November 1874

[In the margin, perpendicular to his own entry, Trollope writes: "Why have I been brought into this edition?"]

(Dodsley, XII, 336) *Worlde and the Chylde* [anonymous]

There is no date earlier for anything else printed in this ed. — excluding John Heywood's plays. How much earlier I cannot tell, nor can Dodsley or his colleagues.

It is strange that so much poetry should be combined with such an innocence of sentiment. May 1880

I have now finished the set.

(Dodsley, XII, 377) *Appius and Virginia* [R.B.]

This is not very good; — not as good for instance as John Heywood's plays, — The Four P's for instance. There is less of wit and not often so excellent a vein of poetry. It seems to have been nearer to a less instructed age. 25 April 1880

Ford, John. *The Works of John Ford.* Ed. by William Gifford and Rev. Alexander Dyce. 3 vols. London: James Toovey, 1869.

(Ford, I, 105) *The Lover's Melancholy*

It must be acknowledged that this is an excellent play, the design being so good and the feeling so excellently portrayed. But yet one feels, almost throughout, that the story is designed rather than well told. One understands what the poet is at, but not from the clearness of his language. There are a few fine passages, chiefly in act IV. The broad comedy is throughout very bad, as it always is with Ford. January 1875

(Ford, I, 208) *'Tis Pity She's A Whore*

The grandeur of some few of the lines makes but poor compensation for the horror of this story and the improbability of the characters. The most striking fault of the piece is that the plot does not at all require that the 'whore's' lover should be her brother. The incest is added on as a makeweight to atrocities which certainly required no such addition. Nothing in fiction, prose or poetry, disgusts so much as unnecessary crime. January 1871

(Ford, I, 319) *The Broken Heart*

Perhaps there is a more continued wail of poetry, a better sustained sadness of romance in this than in any other of Ford's plays. But the language, tho full of poetry, is pompous, and one never in reading it feels a touch of nature. The characters are as unreal as the names and the story — Penthea's woe is on the whole preferable to either the vengeance of Orgilus or the ambition of Ithocles. 31 January 1875

(Ford, II, 108) *Love's Sacrifice*

Nothing could be worse than the whole of this. [No date]

(Ford, II, 217) *Perkin Warbeck*

This play, in having been likened to Shakespeare's work has I think received more praise than it deserves. It is undoubtedly a well written tragedy, in which the characters are carried through with truth and precision. There is also very much poetry in it, though never of a touching kind. But it is dull & heavy, and too manifestly mechanical. And then there are attempts at humour which are vile failures, — as such attempts by Ford always are. January 1875

(Ford, II, 321) *The Fancies Chaste and Noble*

The above criticism is in the main just, but hardly marks sufficiently the continued obscurity of the plot. The teller of stories was even less able to tell his story than Ford. The reader constantly finds himself striving to be at one with the author's mind, and as constantly failing. Ford himself was doubtless aware that it was so. He was evidently straining himself between his love of grand language, and his incapacity to use grand language with simple effects. When he makes the effort his language is almost always fine; — but very rarely rises higher. 28 February 1875

(Ford, III, 98) *The Lady's Trial*

The praise given in the above note, which I suppose to come from Dyce, is for the most part deserved. All the incidents of the play are absurd. The plot is beyond measure ridiculous. There is no reason for anything that is done. But then the characters are all well-handled, the language is good, there is much real poetry, and the comic parts are not grossly offensive as they are so generally with the dramatists of James I. 7 July 1876

(Ford, III, 169) *The Sun's Darling* [(cr. De, IV, 344)]

There is some very pretty poetry in this, which however requires much patience for the perusal. There seems to have been a deal of patience in these days, in writing, in reading, and above all in listening. January 1875

(Ford, III, 271) *The Witch of Edmonton* [(cr. De, IV, 427)]

There is a grandly heavy melancholy about this play, — about even its most comic parts, which gives it a peculiar interest of its own. There is too, in one or two passages, a grand indignation in Mother Sawyer which I cannot agree with Dyce in thinking to be out of place. I cannot think Mother Sawyer to be in any way inferior to Canidia. January 1875

Greene, Robert. *The Dramatic Works of Robert Greene*. Ed. by Rev. Alexander Dyce. 2 vols. London: William Pickering, 1831.

(Greene, I, 53-54) *Orlando Furioso*

There is some very fine poetry, much very bad fun, and a touch here and there of excellent bombast in this very singular piece. The poetry, which in a few passages rises so high as to make one doubt in what work of the old dramatists it is to be beaten except in Shakespeare, — in the earlier part of this work. June 1876

(Greene, I, 214) *Friar Bacon and Friar Bungay* [compare (Do, VIII, 240)]

Read 4 January 1871 — See Dodsley
The mixture of fine poetry and of absolute nonsense in this play is very strange. The marvel is that Shakespeare should have been so infinitely above his contemporaries in imagining scenes, and in writing language, fit for after ages. Greene was no doubt a scholar and a poet; but his works are now caviar to the general. January 1871

81

(Greene, II, 128, 152) *James the Fourth*

[Though Trollope leaves no end comment and no date for this play, he does make two detailed notes on the footnotes. In each he invokes Collier's "Seven Lectures by Coleridge" and in each he is referring to the history of a word or phrase. In the first, it is "dagger" and in the second it is the phrase "loveless love" which he thinks should be "lawless love".]

(Greene, II, 205) *The Pinner of Wakefield* [compare (Do, III, 48)]

Read 2 January 1871 — See Dodsley
There is much life and movement in George-a-Greene; but it by no means equals Roister Doister in nature or language; nor Gammer Gurton's needle in wit. It is free from the vulgarity of the latter. January 1870 [sic, in Halliwell (p. 107) Trollope writes: "Dodsley, Greene's works, Read 2 Jany. 71"]

Hawkins, Thomas, ed. *The Origin of the English Drama.* 3 vols. Oxford, 1773. [The Folger has only volume I.]

(Hawkins, I, 26) *Candlemas Day or the Killing of the Children of Israel* [anonymous]

This is interesting as describing the reformation [?] prejudices, ignorance, and teachings of the times. But there is nothing in it of poetry and very little of expression. August 1882

(Hawkins, I, 68) *Everyman* [anonymous]

There is more in this than in "The Killing of Children," more of expression and of poetry. But still it is very bald. It is odd that there should be nothing in it of Chaucer's richness; — coming even so long after Chaucer. August 1882

(Hawkins, I, 111) *Hycke-Scorner* [anonymous]

A great improvement on Everyman; — not in poetry, at which however there are some attempts; — but in wit and liveliness. August 1882

(Hawkins, I, 163) *Lusty Juventus* [Wever]

Chiefly remarkable for the easy way in which the youth is turned hither and thither by the virtues and vices. And also by the termination shewing that a theatrical entertainment in those days was ordered, and as is litany on a sermon by some form of prayer for the Royal Family. August 1882

(Hawkins, I, 242) *Gammer Gurton's Needle* [Still?; see (Do, II, 83)]

See copy in Dodsley's edition. July 1870

(Hawkins, I, 317) *A Lamentable Tragedy of Cambises King of Persia* [Preston]

Cambysis' vein has not in it much of poetry, whatever it may have of spirit. The royal manner in which he is treated by all around is ridiculous [?]. Hawkins is mistaken in supposing that it was written after Gammer Gurton's Needle. Ambidexter has fun of earlier Rat the Doctor, — or than Merry greke which is between these — in Ralph Roister Doister. September 1882

Heywood, Thomas. *The Dramatic Works.* 6 vols. London: John Pearson, 1874.

(Heywood, I, 90) *First Part of King Edward the Fourth*

A great deal of good home-spun wit, and also good home-spun sense. There is some pretty poetry on Mistress Shore before the king has his way with her, but a great falling off afterwards.

The play I find to be very much better than the criticisms on it given in the Memoirs. January 1875

(Heywood,I,187) *The Second Part of King Edward the Fourth*

Very readable and true to nature, with, every now and then a beautiful line.

> "'Tis our right
> "That wings the body of composed war"

&

> "Nay, beat the spaniell and his master moans"

and

> If it [be] treason for her husband then,
> In the dear bowels of his former love
> To bury his own wrong and her misdeed.

The reader is struck in all the Elizabethan dramatists by the awe felt for the crown, but more so in Heywood than in any. There is no symptom of feeling against Edward for having seduced Jane Shore. 1875

[On p. 143, Catesby yells "A staff, a staff, a thousand crownes for a staff!" and Trollope marks the passage with an X and then writes at the bottom of the page: "This must be a parody on A horse, a horse, my kingdom for a horse"]

(Heywood, I, 247) *If You Know Not Me, You Know Nobody; or The Troubles of Queen Elizabeth*

This is but a poor chronicle; but there are a few lines that interest, — such as that respecting the first English bible on the preceding page. January 1875

(Heywood, I, 344) *Second Part of If You Know Not Me*

This but a poor chronicle, — not nearly so good as that of Ed. IV. The present name shews that it had become popular under some appellation now not known, and shows also how small a joke would catch the people. It was after the same fashion that 'Greens Tu Quoque' was named.

One learns from the piece what were the incidents of Elizabeths reign most popular and most thought of at the end of it. The episode of Dr. Parry is very bad; as indeed is the whole account of the Armada. January 1875

(Heywood, II, 87) *The Faire Maide of the Exchange*

Very poor. By no means equal to Ed. IV. There is a certain homeliness of style about the piece which is pleasant, and a thoroughly English flavour.

The absurdity of the action need hardly be noticed, as the play goers of those days cared nothing for that. That the incidents topple one on another and the language be strong was every thing to them. January 1875

(Heywood, II, 157) *Woman Killed with Kindness* [(cr. Do, VII, 289)]

There are passages in the play so very good, — those in which the injured husband deals with his injury and with his false wife, — as to make it quite remarkable for its excellence among dramas of the kind. Nothing is so wonderful in these pieces as the variations from the top to the bottom of literary excellence, and the little notice which is taken by the Editors of either the goodness or the badness. One cannot but add that the editing of all these plays published by Pearson is below contempt. 31 October 1878

(Heywood, II, 254) *The Four Prentises of London* [(cr. Do, VI, 486)]

This is very poor stuff, only interesting as shewing the sort of matter that pleased the people at the time. No doubt the London prentices were gratified in being told that they were fit to be turned into knights. No audience could now sit through so tedious a performance. January 1875

(Heywood, II, 332) *The Faire Maid of the West: or, a Girl Worth Gold, Part One*

This play is readable, and that is all that can be said for it. It is spoilt by too much haste. 30 May 1880

(Heywood, II, 423) *Faire Maid, Part Two*

An egregiously bad play. One cannot conceive how an audience can have stood its absurdities and its long harshness [?]. But yet from time to time there breaks out a gleam of poetry that almost redeems it. But in the would-be comedy there is no redeeming power. 27 October 1880

(Heywood, III, 79) *The Golden Age*

It is wonderful that so much of mythological story should be pushed into the form of a play and made readable — the love making of Jupiter both to Calisto and Danae is very good. 24 November 1879

(Heywood, III, 164) *The Silver Age*

The story of Amphytrion is the best among the fables collected in this piece, but Moliere tells [?] this with such infinitely finer humour 50 years later as to have taken all the wind out of Heywood's sales [sic]. 28 November 1879

(Heywood, III, 256) *The Brazen Age*

There are some fine passages in this strange [?] tedious play. Aurora's address /p.229/ — Cloris strewing the couch of Venus /p. 235/ — and Hercules describing Omphale /p.242/ are all good. The marvel is that in such a work the author should so well have sustained his effort. 30 November 1879

(Heywood, III, 345) *First Part of the Iron Age*

The continuation and progress of these scenes are wonderful. The strength of the poetry increases as they go on. 4 December 1879

(Heywood, III, 431-32) *The Iron Age Part Two*

The scheme of these 5 plays, or 25 acts for it matters not how they be divided, is elaborate and wonderful; — no less than to combine all the old mythological stories from the birth of Jupiter down to the wanderings of Ulysses, including the giant and Danae and Perseus and Hercules and Proserpine and Jason, with the loves of Mars and Venus, the story of Philoctetes, the whole history of Troy and the tragedies of Orestes, in one long-continued drama. And the poet has so done it that it is all readable, and has thrown into it throughout passages of grand poetry. I look upon Heywood's Ages as one of the marvels of literature. No reader knows them now. The so-called editing of the book is a disgraceful falsehood. 7 December 1879

(Heywood, IV, 95) *The English Traveller* [compare (Di, VI, 218)]

This is a very good play, though much marred by the hurry with which the playwrights of the time go through their work. There is a pathos in it, and poetry, and an excellent though ill-managed plot. The underplot of the Lionels is extravagant and absurd, — but required no doubt, for the delight of the groundlings. 8 February 1880

(Heywood, IV, 164) *A Mayden-head Well Lost*

A worse play never was planned or written. 2 October 1880

(Heywood, IV, 260) *The Witches of Lancashire*

This is very poor stuff. 11 December 1879

(Heywood, V, 78) *A Challenge for Beauty* [virt. id. (Di, VI, 424)]

The plot or two plots of this play are irregular and impossible, but there is some fine poetry and the reader finds that he has something to satisfy him. This is generally the case with Thomas Heywood when he works in a hurry. He composes a fine bit here and there but cannot give himself time to finish his play. Indeed he hardly cares to do so, so long as he may get paid.

> "No nation, sex, complexion, birth degree
> "But jest at want and mock at misery and
> "Unkind man, — thou hast killed me!"

All this is fine. But Isabella and her husband are absurd. 19 April 1880

(Heywood, V, 160) *Love's Mistress* [compare (B, II, xxiv)]

See Baldwin's [sic] Old Plays vol. 2. There is very much excellent poetry in Love's Mistress, and it is perhaps as good a burlesque as there is in the language. It is perhaps the best work we have of Heywood — (T).

The author has introduced a large number of quaint mythological stories, and has sometimes done so with infinite humour. May 1870

(Heywood, V, 257) *The Rape of Lucrece* [virtually identical (B, I, iv)]

This play is thoroughly bad and weak and the wonder is that any critic should say as much for it as is said above (see Baldwin's [sic] Old Plays vol. 1). The character of Lucrece is tame and priggish, nor is there a single fine line put into her mouth. The song "To give my love good morrow" is the best thing in the play. May 1870

(Heywood, V, 353) *The Wise-woman of Hogsdon*

A very poor play indeed, in which the author has not taken the trouble so to digest his plot as to be able to immerse [?] it in the writing.

But if it is badly written it is worse edited. The Editor has supposed that by not altering the manuscripts [?] of some early edition, he will be supposed to have perpetuated the real work. 26 May 1880

(Heywood, VI, 83) *The Royall King and Loyall Subject* [compare (Di, VI, 321)]

There is an absence of life in this play which makes it cold throughout although the plot has been elaborated. The king with whom we cannot sympathise is put above everything, so as to be inhuman, and the husband and [?] Marshal is a male Griselda. 16 March 1880

Jonson, Ben. *The Works of Ben Jonson.* 9 vols. London: Bickers and Son, 1875.

(Jonson, I, cliii) [Gifford's biographical sketch of Jonson]

[Gifford writes: "Long after the period of which we are now speaking, we seldom hear of the eminent characters of the day in their domestic circles; they constantly appear at coffee-houses, which had usurped the place of ordinaries; and it was not till the accession of the present royal family, which brought with it the stability of internal peace, that the mansions of the middle class received those advantages which made home the centre of social as well as of individual happiness and comfort." In the margin beside this, Trollope writes "PSHA!"]

(Jonson, I, cxcii-cxciii) [Gifford's biographical sketch of Jonson]

This biography is full of eulogistic absurdities and angry partisan denunciations. Gifford so loved Jonson that he almost hated Shakespeare, and regarded Marston Dekker & others almost as fiends.

Nothing in this piece has struck me more than the biographer's acknowledgement of one fault, — or rather sin, — in his author. Jonson, he tells us, did not treat the scriptures profanely, but he did fools name and therefore did well to "repent with honour." But Shakespeare, he declares is the "coryphaeus" of profanation. I can hardly understand that with an author so modern as Gifford, who edited the Quarterly in my time, the colloquial and common uses of phrases taken from holy names should have seemed to require "repentance with honour," — an unmeaning and foolish practice which has sprung up in all countries with reference to names permanent in all religions, — while ill-blood calumny, drunkenness & extravagance excite hardly regret.

Of Jonson it may be said that he was an ill-natured critic of others, thinking too much of his own Greek, (as many have done in these days;) — that he was limited in creative power, and dependent on others, not only for plots but also for ideas; — but that he was studious, of great intelligence, finely ambitious, and endowed with great appreciation of character. 29 November 1875

(Jonson, I, 150-51) *Every Man in His Humour*

I cannot find in this comedy the merit with which Gifford credits it. But of all Editors, Gifford is the most pretentiously laudatory. I can understand that the play was well fitted for the stage in its own day. It has more life in acting than in reading. The plot or plots are altogether without interest. There are some few fine lines of poetry, but very few. In spite of Gifford Bobadill is, I think, inferior to Parolles Bessus or Therso [?]. The jealousy of Kitely is most unnatural; — more so even than that of Ford. December 1875

(Jonson, I, 150) *Every Man in His Humour* [a second comment]

I think this a poor play, — by no means equal to the Alchemist. It has been recommended to play-goers by the character of Bobadill, of which humour there is not much, and that not over good. The Kitely jealousy is uninteresting and unintelligible. June 1882

(Jonson, II, 197) *Every Man Out of His Humour*

This is a collection of humorous characters who are supposed to entertain us with their wit rather than a comedy. It has no plot, and no beginning action or catastrophe. The allusions belong so strictly to the time and apply so little to human nature generally that it is often unintelligible. It is full of wit, and the characters are as consistent as they are absurd and disagreeable. The chorus of Cordatus and Mitis is, to my thinking, an abominable interference, — a continual [words illegible] on the part of the author which I cannot imagine to have been popular with the audience at any time. There is in truth but one female character and she is the worst in the piece. December 1875

(Jonson, II, 362) *Cynthia's Revels*

I hardly know how to trust myself with criticism on this piece, which I cannot call a play. For the delectation of any one it is now altogether inept. There are two or three morsels of fine writing, but not enough to leven [sic] such a mass of dough. These passages are almost confined to Crites, by whom we are forced to suppose that Jonson intended himself.

"Here stalks me by a proud and spangled sir" Act III sc.ii, is certainly very good, but then there is very little of it.

As for plot there is none. Even Gifford declares it to be invisible, though he elsewhere says that it is made to stand still. I cannot agree with him that the characters are well-drawn. The most that can be said of them is that the vices they typify are well described; — and even this is too much as the very descriptions are far-fetched. The reader is specially struck by the constant borrowing of thoughts, images, and even passages from Latin poets. The writers of the Elizabethan and subsequent ages all borrowed without sense of shame, thinking it well to get a good thing wherever it was to be found; — but of words and thoughts there was no such borrower as Jonson. The self-conceit of the man as shown in the character of Crites and in the Epilogue is marvellous. There is no wonder that his brothers, Dekker, Chapman and others, attacked him. His flattery of Elizabeth, though gross, is to be excused by the manner of the times.

But criticism on Cynthia's Revels is wasted. The work will have no future readers, unless it be some additional Editors or determined idler like myself. Xmas day 1875

(Jonson, II, 470) *Poetaster* [after Act IV]

How unlike the scene in Romeo and Juliet from which it is taken and how inferior!

Jul. I have forgot why I did call thee back.
Romeo. Let me stand here till thou remember it.
Juliet. I shall forget, to have thee still stand there,
Remembering how I love thy company.

But Jonson could do no love scene, though he did not scruple to copy one, — execrably. July 1882

(Jonson, II, 523-24) *Poetaster*

We are told that the satyre was provoked. We do know its cruel, if not foul, severity; but we do not know the provocation.

There can be little doubt that Dekker is meant by Crispinus and Marston by Demetrius Fannius. Dekker's head of hair as seen in the acknowledged portrait of the poet, is signified when Cloe [sic] says to Crispinus, "Yet, if you can change your head of hair, pray do." Nevertheless we are told by Gifford that Dekker had sustained the hand of Demetrius. Gifford, who was usually as correct as he was bitter, made a mistake here.

As a play the Poetaster is full of matter, as Jonson always is full. There is wit, grandness of language, above all erudition, and a decided purpose. But the wit is often only of the day, the language becomes grandiose (as with Caesar & Virgil) and then Jonson is illnatured.

To show that he was not ashamed of translating, — with which he had been twitted, — Jonson translates two entire satires of Horace. That on the Roman bore [words illegible], he brings in fairly well. It is not needed as a part of the play, but it passes. The other, Saint Crispins in Salina, is brought in neck and heels, and cannot be said to be a part of the play at all.

One is driven to fear that Jonson could bear no brother near the throne, and that he was driven, not by envy of those above him, but by malice toward those who came near his heels, to tear in pieces his hopeful rivals.

There is great wit in the Poetaster, and the play interests me specially as giving us a true picture of the feuds which raged among the poets of the day.

Shakespeare was too great to talk on anything of this. December 1875

(Jonson, II, 510) *Poetaster* [yet another comment]

On again reading this I do not find it very good. There is much in it that is — I am sure bad. The translation from Virgil is, in spite of Gifford's apology, very poor. The most remarkable thing in it is the extent of

Jonson's reading of the classics as is here displayed. His intimacy with his authors surpasses that of most scholars of today. July 1882

(Jonson, III, 152-53) *Sejanus*

It would perhaps be unfitting to call Sejanus a fine tragedy, but it contains more of tragic poetry than anything I know in the English language out of Shakespeare; and has more matter in it, than, perhaps, any play written by Shakespeare.

The cleverness [?] of Jonson's mind and the strength of his intelligence has perhaps been somewhat kept in abeyance by the infinitely greater sweetness and perspicacity of Shakespeare's verses, and by that great man's better command of words.

The learning displayed in Sejanus is very great, but the work shows itself to have been hurried. Jonson too often condescends simply to translate passages from the authors who have been his authorities. The grander passages of the play are, nevertheless, his own. (No) November 1875

[Beside Sejanus's long speech, Act II.ii. (p. 49) "No/ They are too great, and that too faint..." Trollope writes: "I know no better example than this in the English language of the weight and dignity and fitness of rhymed verse for dramatic tragic poetry."]

(Jonson, III, 153) *Sejanus* [a later opinion]

The men of this play, — Sejanus, all walk about like men & [?] Romans. It is a tragedy, complete as to its tragedy and yet containing as a tragedy should numerous odd bits of comedy. But it contains no woman's part. And the grander parts are made up of translated morsels. No great English writer ever shewed so complete a knowledge of a foreign language.

As is generally the case with Jonson the interest is gone before the fourth act is finished. The "grander epistles" [?] is rubbish. August 1882

(Jonson, III, 323) *The Fox*

With all Jonson's plays the plot falls off at the end. Here the continuing of the plot is good, but the consummation is wretched. There is no word for the punishments awarded except that they have been deserved. The three first acts are excellent; but are much injured [?] by the extent of Giffords praise. July 1882

[In a note on p. 301 Gifford lauds Lady Would-be "...and it would be an absolute defect of understanding, to place any... by the side of..." and Trollope writes "Oh,Oh!!"]

(Jonson, III, 324) *Volpone*

With Cumberland I hold this to be the best of Jonson's plays. The wit of the dialogue, the learning displayed, and the ingenuity of the plot as discovered in the first four acts, are excellent. But Gifford, who is not contented with Cumberland's praise, says boldly that it is the greatest thing ever done in comedy. When one remembers Meredemius [?], Jaques & Rosalind, Tartuffe, and Sir Peter Teazle, (whom I imagine Gifford did not know) one is obliged to smile at the Editor's enthusiasm.

Indeed the comedy of Jonson is never good. It is excellent satire, but as comedy is not sufficiently life-like. And here in the Fox, the plot falls off so much toward the end, when it should become plain, and so dwindles from neglect down to nothing, that the reader, while enjoying the satire, is obliged to confess that the play is imperfect. 26 December 1875

(Jonson, III, 482) *The Silent Woman*

To my thinking the Silent Woman is inferior both in plot and character to the Fox and The Alchemist. It must be owned that the solution of the difficulty is well hidden to the last. The reader does not expect it. I cannot imagine that a spectator should at all have understood the circumstances which led to it; — certainly not the excuses for a divorce, which are given in Latin. But the care with which the plot is wrapped up tends itself to produce tedium. One does not see an end to the perpetual fooling. Dryden's praise is based on grounds which to me are naught. I never think of asking how many days are taken in "As You Like It," or even quarrel with "A Winter's Tale" because of the lapse of time. Who really now loves a play the better because all the scenes are laid in two contiguous houses, — except the proprietor who has to furnish the properties? That feeling is over.

The play is full of strong writing, no doubt, — and of wit; but it is confused and tedious. Nor can I allow it to be to the praise of an author that all the best of this work is taken from other authors. Sure there never was such a plagiarist as Jonson! January 1876

[On p. 458 Gifford quotes Whalley's note faulting Jonson's "too bold" introduction of phrases from the learned languages. Gifford drags in Shakespeare to say he does it, too, and Trollope writes in pencil: "Had any one said that Jonson squinted, Gifford would have sworn that Shakespeare look[ed] across with both eyes — "]

(Jonson, IV, 181-82) *The Alchemist*

The Alchemist is certainly a very great work. It is full of wit, learning, and satire. But the reader is constrained by Gifford's idolatry to quarrel with the work. This play is a great satire, but not a great comedy. Jonson never achieves a woman's part. He hardly even tries to make a woman charming. They are all whores or fools — generally both. Gifford expatiates continually on the universality of Jonson's reading. I cannot but express an opinion that Jonson wrote up to his erudition, instead of illustrating his writing by his erudition. Others have done it since, — as no doubt did others before; — but it is to be found in all that Jonson did. A writer dips into a wide mass of literature, and then uses what he finds. The mass with Jonson was very wide; but twas so he used it. One constantly finds the taste of his last studies, — often of Horace, often of Juvenal, sometimes of some English work. But in truth Gifford has injured Jonson by his wide-mouthed praise. January 1876

(Jonson, IV, 182-83) *The Alchemist* [second comment]

Nothing is more provoking than Gifford's exorbitant praise of this play. It is very clever; the plot is well arranged; the dialogue is always amusing, and the language never descends to mediocrity[?]. The knowledge shewn of all the vulgar tricks of the alchemists dirty trade is amazing, and proves the reading of Jonson to have been amazing. But it is dirty, vulgar, and disgusting without ceasing for one act, one scene, one passage, or one line. Filth was common to the dramatists of James I; but here there is nothing but filth. Mammon rises to poetry in the the [sic] description he gives of the pleasures of lewdness and grossness. But he only so rises. There are two women; one more nastily spoken [?] than men, and the other more foolish. No one but Jonson could have written a play, in which no character is not an arrant, brutal knave. But none but Jonson could have made all his arrant brutal knaves so witty. January 1882

(Jonson, IV, 183) *The Alchemist* [third comment]

I have again read the play, now for the third, or probably fourth time, and I cannot much alter the criticism written 1876. As a play it is not dramatic. As a narrative it is hardly poetic. There are grand bits of narrative, that of Pertinax towards the close being the finest. But here the praise quoted from Whalley as to the poets originality is hardly correct. May 1882

(Jonson, IV, 336) *Catiline*

I regard this as the heaviest play I know in the English language. Though the subject be greater than that of Sejanus, it is less tragic and less open to poetry. Jonson has stuck so close to the historians that the work is historical rather than dramatic. His translations are so close that he rarely rises to poetry, Cicero is the leading personage of the play; but he is the dullest. There is nothing in the whole piece so free as a word or two from Juvenal on the same subject, —

> Sed; Roman parentem,
> Roma Patrem Patria Ciceronem libera disit.

Jonson has endeavoured to enliven the learning of his play by the characters of Fulvia and Sempronia. He is never fortunate with his women — These are nasty, — and the reader is thankful that he has but little of Fulvia who reeks from a brothel. January 1876.

(Jonson, IV, 510) *Bartholomew Fair*

It is difficult in speaking of plays of the time of James I to estimate the difference of taste of an audience of that time and of ours. The tedious fun of the scenes at Bart. Fair, which would now be intolerable on the stage, was probably liked in its day and if so is entitled to the praise of readers success. But as works of art we can compare Jonson's plays with others of the same date, — and in doing so Bartholomew Fair seems to me to be very poor indeed. It is coarse and ugly throughout. The wit is ponderous and the characters overstrained.

Gifford takes credit for the feminine virtues of Grace Welborn. She has very little part to play; a bit, when desirous of breaking from a disagreeable engagement, she does so by tossing up which she shall take of two strange suitors. February 1876

(Jonson, V, 148-49) *The Devil is an Ass*

Amusing and light-in-hand, but coarse and sometimes very absurd. The author has again failed in the woman's part, as he does always. She is half-whore at first, and after that she is nothing. March 1876

The best scene in the comedy, — and that is very good, — is the discourse which Wittipol makes to the lady in the husband's presence, when he and the lady meet at the opposite windows. The song which Wittipol sings before her husband comes is the prettiest bit of melody in any play of Jonson's. Act II sc.ii.

(Jonson, V, 293-94) *The Staple of News*

This play is unintelligible in some parts, very far-fetched in others, replete with allegories mixed up with realities, and tiresome with its absurdities. The author seems to have intended at first a satire against the dominant taste for news, and then to have been run away with by the much easier task of satirising a love of money. But some very fine lines have been put into the mouth of the canter. For instance, — in the last scene;

> "Superstition
> Does violate the deity it worships
> No less than scorn does."

In which passage Ben Jonson surely wrote 'worshipeth' though the word is not so given in any of the Editions I have.
And again

> "For sparrow with his little plumage flies,
> "While the proud peacock overcharged with pens
> "Is fain to sweep the ground with his grown tail [sic, grountrain]
> "And load of feathers."

March 1876

(Jonson, V, 414) *The New Inn*

Gifford's apology* is so touching that even at this distance of time the critic cannot criticise. May 1876

[*Gifford (p. 414) says that Jonson was too sick to write at all but clung to the hope that he really was writing better than he thought himself able: "—the fact seems to be, that poor Jonson, though his faint and faltering tongue could scarcely shake out a few lines...."]

(Jonson, VI, 118) *The Magnetic Lady*

No play of Ben Jonson's is more Jonsonian than this. The purport of the humour is, as usual, very difficult to understand. Sometimes I think I have it, and then again that I am astray. The boy in the interludes does not improve the matter at all. He only answers the criticisms on various points, which of course are so made as to be easily answered.

Why Magnetic Lady? Why Compass? Why Ironside? Why Needle? Needle as to tailor is well enough, but here there is reference to the magnetic needle. The man is steward rather than tailor.

The plot is very poor; — in which it is presumed that the aunt will at the end be quite satisfied that the servant girl is her real niece, and the supposed niece of 18 years only a serving girl and a ⎯⎯⎯⎯. But affection goes for nothing with Jonson.

The personages are all displeasing as well as unintelligible in their humours. Why is the cleverest piece in the play put into the mouth of Sir Diaphanous who is supposed to be a foolish courtier? For there is nothing so good as his description of the various sorts of courage. Polish with her volubility and resources is the best character. 5 May 1876

(Jonson, VI, 226) *A Tale of a Tub*

There can, I think, be no doubt that Jonson, in his Tale of a Tub, tried to produce effects which were beyond his reach. There is every now and then a bit of bombastic verse in which the personage on the stage begins to tell mean things in magniloquent words; — a kind of drollery which was then common and is still popular; but it is not continued sufficiently in any scene to justify us in thinking it was more than a temporary attempt — I fear that the predominant feeling on reading the play is that the author had spent his fire and was extracting what heat he could from the embers.

The peculiar mode of attack against contemporaries which was common in Jonson's time and which seems to have peculiarly recommended itself to him has never been made more apparent than in the ridicule through out this piece on Inigo Jones, whom Jonson probably disliked only as a rival in getting up Court masques.

There is a certain amount of fun in the Tale of a Tub, which pleases even to this day; — but chiefly I think because it has to do with places the names of which are so well known to us as Kentish Town, Pancras, and Tottenham Court Road. 1 June 1876

(Jonson, VI, 288) *The Sad Shepherd*

To say that the Sad Shepherd, had it come to us entire, would have been a poem superior "to the proudest effort of dramatic genius which time has bequeathed us" is an absurdity that could have come only from Gifford, — But that which we have of it, as a lyrical drama, is so sweet as to make me think that it is the greatest effort of Jonsons muse. As I have before been led by certain of the poets songs, so am I now induced by this piece, to think that dramatic description of rural charm, of rural life, and of scenery, — also of rural fun and joke, was Jonsons greatest power. I think that he was led to town life, to old story, and to satyre by his

96

reading, and by a certain desire to shine; but it is in his rusticnesses, his masques, his songs, and his underwoods that the poet appears at his best. 2 June 1876

(Jonson, VI, 396-97) *The Case is Altered*

This play, which no doubt is by Jonson is very unlike Jonson's work. There is more dependence on on [sic] the plot and less on the language than is to be found in any of the later pieces; — and so in borrowing from Marston he takes the plots but does not translate many passages.

One is led to hope at first that the characters of Rachel and Aurelia will be exceptions to Jonson's ordinarily insipid women; but they do not make good their promise. There is no touching expression of love. Rachel no doubt is constant and good, but she is constant and good in a wooden fashion. Perhaps Juniper [a cobbler] and Onion [a groom] have the best of it, which is not saying much for the play. 27 February 1876

(Jonson, VI, 455) *The Satyr*

Feb. 25 76

[Trollope responds to another of Gifford's footnotes (p. 443) in this play. Malone said there were no triplets in Shakespeare's time. Gifford lashes back "To go no further; there are at least half a dozen instances in this little piece. But Mr. Malone was grossly ignorant of Jonson: ignorance, however, is but a wretched apology for calumny." Trollope writes in the margin: "Where is the calumny?"]

Marlowe, Christopher. *The Works of Christopher Marlowe.* Ed. by Rev. Alexander Dyce. 3 vols. London: William Pickering, 1850.

(Marlowe, I, 226) *Second Part of Tamburlaine the Great*

The first & second parts of Tamburlaine are I think the finest of Marlowe's work. The magnificence of the language is often so great as to cast into shadow the terrible defects of sentiment, & the roll of the poetry is often so fine as to convince the reader of the presence of something sublime. But as these plays are finer than the others, so are they more turgid; and there is in them the same absence of all sweetness which renders every work of Marlowe harsh. There is nothing of love, — & seldom a single character with whom the reader can sympathise. In Tamburlaine there is not one. 1 January 1868

(Marlowe, I, 349) *The Jew of Malta* [(cr. Do, VIII, 327)]

There is neither pathos nor tenderness in this piece. And the incidents are so improbable, incongruous and ill devised as to render the story wholly uninteresting. But there is a certain power of language which carries the reader on, and which is the shrewd characterisation of the Elizabethan dramatists and the only claim of many of them. 24 November 1867

(Marlowe, II, 84) *The Tragical History of Doctor Faustus* [compare (Di, I, 88)]

I remember well my reading of this play 30 years since — and seeing [?] it then to be full of grand poetry. I now find the fine passages to be few — & very short. The speech to Helen's ghost is the finest. And the quick falling down from poetic height to the absurdest and most grovelling language is such as to leave a final judgment very much against the work. Marlowe never creates a feeling of sympathy. With his Faustus no one cares whether the Devil has him or no. 2 December 1867

(Marlowe, II, 290) *Edward the Second* [(cr. Do, II, 404)]

It is said that this was considered to be, in a dramatist's point of view, the best of Marlowe's plays. We can hardly understand this now, so tedious is it from its length, — to the feeling of which perhaps there is some addition by its not being broken into acts. There is much fine language in the play, especially in the latter half, but there is not a single character which can excite sympathy, whereas the whining of the king for his man-friend, the fickleness of the Queen, and the cruelty of Mortimer are disgusting. The author has not understood how to throw many years into one piece, so as not to rob the action of his personages of an appearance of rational consequence. 1 December 1867

(Marlowe, II, 359) *The Massacre at Paris*

This is sad trash and unworthy of Marlowe of whom it may be said that though his characters are uninteresting his poetry is often grand. There is hardly a fine line in this, — which has indeed been written so hurriedly that the very rhythm often halts. As a rule Marlowe's ear is correct, and his versification though monotonous is sonorous.

This play is furnished [?] of the events of some twenty years in the history of France put together in a dramatic form — as was usual with the Elizabethan Dramatists, but with total absence of dramatic effect. 4 June 1876

(Marlowe, II, 439) *Dido, Queen of Carthage* [verbatim (B, II, xiv)]

This burlesque on Dido's story as told by Virgil is pretty, quaint, and graceful. It can hardly be called a play though the ending is tragical enough. It was probably to a much greater degree the work of Nash than of Marlowe. 26 June 1870

[It is interesting to note that many of the pages in this play are uncut.]

Marston, John. *The Works of John Marston.* Ed. J. O. Halliwell. 3 vols. London: John Russell Smith, 1856.

(Marston, I, 68-69) *First Part of Antonio and Mellida* [compare (Di; II, 191)]

It is almost inconceivable that so bad a play should have lived so long and enjoyed a reputation. It is bad in plot, in language, and in character. The plot is as a whole altogether without meaning. Now and again a line or two occurs which is worth preserving — as for instance;

> As having crushed a rose —
> Within my palm, the rose being ta'en away
> My hand retains a little breath of sweet.

9 January 1871

(Marston, I, 144) *Antonio's Revenge*

Another bad play, crowded with loud-mouthed bombast, confused, and most uninteresting. There are in it two passable imitations from Shakespeare — Andrugio rising as a ghost to excite his son to vengeance, and Antonio's acting the fool taken from Lear. Both are handled wretchedly. A certain grandness of sound is Marston's chief recommendation, — a gratification which seems to have gone a long way in his time. 24 June 1874

(Marston, I, 215) *The Tragedie of Sophonisba*

This, the finest of Marston's plays, has so much of true [two words illegible] poetry, as to entitle it to the name of a great work. But it is often unintelligible; and sometimes so ill composed as to leave the idea that the author did not himself always know what he intended to express. 22 November 1879

99

(Marston, I, 218) *What You Will* [compare (Di, II, 290)]

Read Oct. 1867

"What You Will" is a good comedy — with some few fine lines — & much humour; but terribly confused, loaded with unnecessary characters, and almost unintelligible in its language. That which seems to be sarcasm on the bombast of other writers is itself so bombastic as to lose the flavour of its wit.

In reading all these plays one wonders at Shakespeare's perspicacity and easiness of language more than at any of his greater gifts.

(Marston, II, 106) *The Fawne* [compare (Di, II, 407)]

There is a great deal of wit, and a little, — but very little — poetry in this play. It seems to have been left by the author in great confusion of language, which has been made, if possible, worse by the Editor who has reprinted all misspellings, as though there were some hidden purpose in them. In all editing of our Tudor and Stuart plays one regrets Dyce when Dyce is absent.

There is some fooling on the word "only" in this play, of which I do not see the exact purpose. 15 November 1879

(Marston, II, 192) *The Dutch Courtezan*

A most foul play, — full of obscenity, ill arranged, crowded with all possible faults that can disgrace a play; — but nevertheless there is in it a certain wit, — and in one or two passages some amount of pathos. 9 January 1870

(Marston, II, 292) *The Malcontent* [written by Webster and augmented by Marston; (cr. Do, IV, 96)]

This is a wonderfully clever play, — coarse, improbable, sometimes disgusting, always irrational, but full of wit, and often of poetry. The four first acts are very good reading; but the play falls off greatly in the fifth act. 8 January 1871 [The date as written by Trollope looks very much like 1874, but Halliwell (p. 162) has 8 Jan 1871 and Dodsley has Jan. 1871.]

(Marston, III, 101-102) *Eastward Hoe* [By Chapman, Jonson, Marston; compare (Do, IV, 279)]

This is a most tedious play, with very little humour, and unworthy of Jonson's name. It is the story, (which was probably current long before) of the diligent and idle apprentices; but even the moral is travestied as at the end the joke consists in the old tradesman being taken in by the mock repentance of the idle one. What a job it must have [word missing], what a cutting of blocks with razors to edit such stuff as this with care, comparing various editions, line by line!

It should be remembered that to the audience much of the delight of many plays of the time, and especially of this one, arose from satire of the day which we only partially understand. Quicksilvers repentance is of this nature, and is thus in some degree justified. 7 June 1873

Massinger, Philip. *The Plays of Philip Massinger.* Ed. by William Gifford. 4 vols. 1805.

(Massinger, I, 121) *The Virgin-Martyr* [(cr. De, IV, 91)]

The poetry in this play is most beautiful. The story-telling is execrable. Such may be said of much of the work of Massinger and his contemporaries. Between Massinger and Dekker in this play I can draw no line. The two would-be comic rascals are abominable. Gifford says, and probably truly, that they are Dekker's; — but in the passages attributed to Dekker there are as fine lines as any in the play, — as for instance; —

> A thousand blessings danced upon his eyes —

April 1876

(Massinger, I, 230) *The Unnatural Combat*

There are some very fine passages in this play, — sufficient to justify a critic in praising it for its poetry, though even in this richest there is a great falling off in the last act, as to which the reader feels that the work has been hurried. But the plot, — or plots are abominable, — not only as being horrid but as being ill-contrived. And, in my judgement, there is nothing in the delineation of character to justify the praises given by Dr. Ireland. April 1876

(Massinger, I, 343-44) *The Duke of Milan*

This is a very good play; — in plot perhaps the best that Massinger ever wrote. And in versification it is very fine. But when the critic comes to talk of Othello he finds the difference. Sforza is not Othello, nor is Francisco even near to Iago, or Marcelia to Desdemona. 29 July 1876

(Massinger, II, 117-18) *The Bondman*

To my taste the beauty of this play consists entirely in the language, the beauty and cadence of which is so great that in the mere gift of ear I am inclined to think that Massinger beat all the dramatists of his time. In the plot I can acknowledge nothing to be good—Who can sympathise with lovers who change their love during the short time of the action, as do Cleon and Leosthenes, or admire a character such as Pisander after he has instigated slaves to commit rapine on unprotected women? We are offended throughout the reading of the play, especially with the exaggerated obscenity of one or two scenes,—as to which the charitable Dean of Westminster merely suggests that they are "stained by obscenity".

Massinger is almost as unable as Ford to be humorous with grace. But the melody of his words is marvellous. April 1876

(Massinger, II, 231) *The Renegado*

The whole thread of the story is abominable and ridiculous. Men and women who have been but now the worst of their kind become suddenly Saints. Turks become Christian under adversity, and no likeness of probability is maintained. Nor can I say that there is a single character in the play which leaves a mark upon the readers mind. There are, however, some fine passages—as that in Act II Scene IV.

> "These knights of Malta" &c.

and Act IV Scene ii

> "Unkind nature
> To make weak women servants—"&c.

But the poetry is inferior to that of Massinger generally,—especially in the last act. He usually falls away at the end of his plays,—not allowing himself sufficient time for elaboration. 21 April 1876

(Massinger, II, 322) *The Parliament of Love*

Much of the former part of this is very pretty, though it be abominably obscene. The last act, with the unravelling of the plot, is tedious beyond expression,—so as to be almost unreadable. 30 April 1876

(Massinger, II, 420-21) *The Roman Actor*

I cannot give this play even so much credit as Dr. Ireland does. The episodes, that is the scenes in which the action acts, are uninteresting, whether they help the plot or no. The Emperor rarely rises to the expression of high poetry, though his character is, I think, the best in the play. Domitia is at first one woman, then a second different from the first, and then a third different from either. The Roman actor himself is never very low, but he never rises very high. I cannot help observing the Dean's statement that Massinger's stage arrangements are generally exact. He is most inexact in such matters, as Gifford himself points out more than once. 29 July 1876

(Massinger, II, 520) *The Great Duke of Florence*

The story here is worth nothing, nor are the characters worth much, though those of Lidia and Giovanni are at first very sweet. But the language of this play is so good, and the poetry in many places is deliciously sweet as to make me feel inclined to place it first after Shakespeare of all the plays of the great era to which it belongs.

It has to be said of the play, — as of many others of the period, — that the author seems to have become tired of it before it was finished, so as not to have maintained his power to the end. 15 July 1876

(Massinger, III, 107) *The Maid of Honour*

Taking this play as a whole I am bound to say that it is very good. I cannot, however, agree in all the old dean's praise. The poetry is often very fine, — often specially melodious, — the characters are well sustained — especially that of Camiola; but the story itself is not only unnatural but very displeasing. The poet too has crammed into his work very much too great a share of action. 28 April 1876

(Massinger, III, 231-32) *The Picture*

This is a most admirable play, — as to which one feels that it is unnecessary to inveigh against the unwomanliness of the Queen or against the assumed virtue of the heroine, — which had so nearly fallen. The whole thing is told so well and the different parts are in characters so charming, that at the end one finds all objections to be hyper criticism — and then the wisdom of it —

    Good; the events — &c.

see page 218 [act V,ii Soph.]

In many places the melody is so charming that one marvels at Massinger's power in adopting words to rhythm — In some others he has taken no such trouble and they are flat enough — 24 June 1876

[At the end of Act I, Trollope writes: "Very good indeed. Honoria most excellent"]

(Massinger, III, 344-45) *The Emperor of the East*

This is a good play and well managed, but it never rises very high. I altogether disagree with the Dean's criticism in as far as it falls foul of the play because the action does not commence till the 4th act. It is one of the chief merits of all these plays that they do not depend on their interest for an incident, but carry on as it were a certain section of life, giving pictures here and there — It required a Shakespeare to combine with this one permeating plot for the whole. 1 August 1876

(Massinger, III, 474-75) *The Fatal Dowry*

The language of this play is beautiful, — often soaring to poetry of the highest order. Gifford complains more than once of cooperation with Field, but I do not find any room for fault. Throughout there is a charm about it which arises from the author's perfect understanding of the nature of the vehicle which he is to use. In this as in all the plays written toward the end of Fletcher's time there is a certain extravagance both of character and plot. Women are whores in one act and are ready to sacrifice their lives to ideas of chastity in the next. Nothing can be more whorish than Beaumelle; — nothing more unnatural than her superb repentance. Men are subjected to the same unnatural repentance. With many of the post-Elizabethan dramatists one has to bargain for this inconsequence. But their language makes full atonement. March 1876

(Massinger, III, 590) *A New Way to Pay Old Debts*

This is an excellent play, — hardly to be called a comedy, as all that is of fine quality in it is tragic in its element. The comic character of Greedy is very poor and monotonous. The character and excellence of the play hangs almost entirely on the great strength of Overreach. I know no personage in the British drama better adapted to bring out the power of a great dramatist. 7 July 1870

[Trollope inserts into the volume a page and a half of his suggested alternatives to words in the play. For example, he suggests "stomach" for the word "belly" in one of Greedy's speeches, and suggests leaving out altogether Greedy's exclamation "Oh, my guts."]

(Massinger, IV, 116) *The City Madam*

The 4 first acts of this play are excellent, — better than anything else that I remember of Massingers as to plot and characters; — with more likeness to life even than Overreach. The poetry also is very good. There is a subtlety about the work that reminds one of Ben Jonson, with more that is natural.

But the falling off in the 5th act is terrible. Gifford attempts to excuse it but has evidently felt it. All likeness to life ceases, and the story becomes grotesquely absurd. 22 April 1876

(Massinger, IV, 232) *The Guardian*

This play is throughout so bad that to sit in judgment on it at all is as Dr Johnson says, as quoted in one of the notes, to "waste criticism in unresisting imbecility." I know nothing worse in the whole range of the old English drama. 1 April 1876

(Massinger, IV, 343) *A Very Woman*

Upon the whole this is a good play, though with many faults of construction [?] — as for instance that Almira should not know her false slave, — which is in itself admissible in accordance with the stage probabilities of that time, — but that she should not know him after he had given his name!

The great fault of the play is in the abominable foul nastiness, and want of wit of the would-be funny characters, Cuculo and Borachio. In such attempts Massinger always failed.

The glory of the play is in one or two magnificent passages, — that especially beginning "This beauty in the blossom of my youth" p. 317 I almost go along with Gifford in the hyper-enthusiasm of his praises for this passage. There are others good, though not equally good. 6 August 1876

(Massinger, IV, 453) *The Bashful Lover*

This again is a bad play, though by no means so bad as The Guardian. But it is weak and unnatural in its story, and for the most part lacks the peculiar sweetness of Massinger's melody. This no doubt came from hurry. The chivalry is as mawkish as that of the old Arcadian Romances, — from which indeed it was taken without that adaptation to common sense which has been usual with British writers when handling such fables. 6 August 1876

(Massinger, IV, 573) *The Old Law* [(cr. Mi, I, 120)]

I think the critics are too hard on the Old Law. The parts written by Massinger chiefly in the 4th-5th acts are clearly discernible, and are very sweet, — as is so much of Massingers poetry. The fun of Middleton (or

Rowley) — for I do not distinguish between them is dirty and common-place, but is often very funny. With old Agatha there is even a touch of true pathos. July 1876

(Massinger, IV, 584) *The Old Law* [another comment]

I know nothing in the business of editing worse in taste than the continued abuse from Gifford of Mason and Coxeter as given in the notes of this work. Being before him they of course had fewer advantages than he — But, — putting that aside, — an editor need not vilify his predecessors, even though they have tumbled into error. Many annotators have been coarse and vituperative; — but Gifford I think has beaten them all. 1876

Middleton, Thomas. *The Works of Thomas Middleton.* Notes by Rev. Alexander Dyce. 5 vols. London: Edward Lumley, 1840.

(Middleton, I, 120) *The Old Law* [see (Mas, IV, 573)]

Read 8 July 1876
See Massinger's works.

(Middleton, I, 222) *The Mayor of Queenborough* [compare (Do, XI, 183)]

This play is very bad reading, but is interesting as showing what a gallimafrey [sic] of plot was pleasing to the frequenters of plays in the reign of James I. There is such a variety of incident that it can all be included in the one piece only by the insertion of dumb shews between the acts, and yet, with even that aid it must have been very long. I cannot but think that it must also have been very tedious.

Simon the Mayor has but very little to do with the play, the connexion between him and the Vortiger plot maintained only by the thongs of leather the mayor cut. He seems to have been introduced simply that the horseplay of the cheaters and the clown might be introduced on the stage. The present name has grown onto the play probably because his portion of the action best pleased the audience. 3 June 1874

(Middleton, I, 308-09) *Blurt, Master-Constable*

It is impossible to criticise this play by any laws of literature as they exist now; — as it is also absurd to judge it by the taste of the present age.

From the days of Marlowe and Shakespeare downwards the dramatists gradually fell from poetry and charm of characters — pointing to quaintness of language and intricacy of plot, garnished with bawdry, till at last they brought plays to the path so garbled in language and so confused in incident as to be almost unintelligible to the reader of the present day. Middleton, who was late among the lot, was about the most offensive. Nevertheless there is in this comedy a certain spirit which makes it readable.

Why it should have been called by the Constable's name I cannot say, unless it had first some other name and then was known by the special acting of one person, as Greene's Tu Quoque and Lord Dundreary in our own time. 29 May 1874

(Middleton, I, 409) *The Phoenix*

This is an intricate uninteresting vulgar play, written altogether for the audience and not for the closet, — and which I should think must have been dull even to an audience. Tangle who goes mad over his loss has the best of it. 17 February 1877

[Beside these early words of the Duke (p. 314): "Experience quickens; travel confirms the man," Trollope writes: "Home staying youths have ever homely wits Two Gent. of Verona"]

(Middleton, I, 514) *Michaelmas Term*

The grains of wheat are so few that it is hard indeed to pick them out of the chaff. There are a few grains, but the chaff is overwhelming. That such a play should ever have pleased a large audience is the marvel. 6 February 1878

(Middleton, II, 99) *A Trick to Catch the Old One* [verbatim (Di, V, 224)]

I cannot call this a good play, though I can understand that it should have been lively on the stage. The fun is all low in its nature, and of poetry there is little or none. As to the morality the less said the better. 15 January 1877

(Middleton, II, 209) *The Family of Love*

The wit of this play, or rather I should say the fun, is much too poor to erase the dullness and the coarseness together. When it breaks into verse the verses are more prosaic than the prose. See the dialogue between Gerardine and Maria Act III sc. 1 than which nothing can be worse. 4 March 1877

(Middleton, II, 323) *Your Five Gallants*

This piece is so tedious, so perplexed so uninteresting and so bad, that one is at [a] loss to conceive how such a man as Dyce could have given up his time to editing it. To have read it is a sin, in the wasting of time. 24 March 1878

(Middleton, II, 422) *A Mad World, My Masters* [(cr. Do, V, 358)]

This is a good rattling comedy of the times, with more of true fun in it than many, — but still without anything in it worthy of notice. It is Middleton, perhaps at his best, — but only Middleton. April 1878

(Middleton, II, 559) *The Roaring Girl* [compare Do, VI, 106); (cr. De, III, 232)]

A most unintelligible gallimafrey [sic], unreadable as a whole and but little worth the labour of the attempt; but with sparkles of such wit as was then popular. It is not divided into acts and therefore the more confused. This and many plays of James I were probably written in great haste to satisfy the demands of the stage. They are hardly worth looking at except as giving pictures of the period. August 1873

In the above note I have spoken of the play as not divided into acts and scenes, — whereas it has been so divided by Dyce, in this volume. But the note is extracted from Dodsley in whose edition I read the play. In Pearsons edition of Dekkers works the piece is again given undivided; but with that work no trouble whatever was taken —

(Middleton, III, 122) *The Honest Whore* [see (De, II, 91); (cr. Do, III, 322)]

See Dekker's works. November 1873

(Middleton, III, 244) *The Honest Whore, Second Part* [see De, II, 183); (cr. Do, III, 425)]

See Dekker's works. December 1873

(Middleton, III, 335) *The Witch*

This play is for the most part confused outrageous and uninteresting, nor is there anything to recommend it to special attention but the fact that it contains certain expressions which make it not improbable that Shakespeare borrowed from it — It may have been written before Macbeth; — though not before Othello, — and there is a passage in Act IV Sc.III which seems to shew that one had must [sic] known the work of the other. There is no other interest in Middletons witch, which is very inferior to the work generally of the Elizabethan dramatists. January 1877

(Middleton, III, 440) *The Widow* [see (BF, IV, 383); (Do, XII, 295)]

Read Nov. 30 1874. See B & F's works Dyce Vol. IV.

(Middleton, III, 549) *A Fair Quarrel*

This is a very good play, but surely Middleton never wrote it. The play, no doubt, was Rowleys with the parts of the rogues and street-walkers put in by Middleton. C. Lamb in his criticism — see p. 293 [sic, 493] — is quite correct as to the excellence of the main plot as shewn in the characters of Ager and Ager's mother, but has not seen or has not been careful to mark, the difference between the work of the two dramatists to whom the play has been attributed. Middleton never did such work as that of the scenes in which Ager is concerned; — never wrote such poetry or conceived such characters. Rowley is called a third rate dramatist; — perhaps correctly if Shakespeare is to form the 1st class and Fletcher the second; — but Rowley was a poet and understood a plot. Middleton only understood the appetite of his audience for low buffoonery. 31 March 1878

(Middleton, III, 645) *More Dissemblers Besides Women* [compare (Di, IV, 428)]

This play like most of Middletons is very hard reading. I can understand that there should have been amusement from the acting, according to the fun of the time there could have been fun in the singing master and the dancing master giving lessons to the poor mock page when she was about to fall in to the straw. And in the dignity of the Duchess and the hypocrisy of the Cardinal there may have been amusement. All the various underplots no doubt served, though each severally is poor. But as a play for the closet there is nothing in it. It never rises to poetry though there is much easy versification. 27 April 1877

(Middleton, IV, 88) *A Chaste Maid in Cheapside*

Middleton's plays are all bad to me. The system on which he plans them disgusts me. Every character here is vitious. — except that of the girl Moll, who consequently has little to do. And then his sudden repentances are as bad as his successful rascals. But all this is not the worst. When he is funny, — in prose, — his fun is always dull. When he rises to poetry — or attempts to rise, he cannot get his feet off the ground. This is the case in this play when the author attempts to become serious. The lines which Moll sing p. 88 [V.ii] would make a pretty song. 31 March 1877

(Middleton, IV, 202) *The Spanish Gipsy* [compare (Di, IV, 218)]

This play is often tedious and sometimes obscure; but there is much in it good in action and something of real poetry. The humour, like all that of Middleton, is poor for this age. It perhaps suited a time in which men were less impatient and more easily pleased. The poetry we may be sure did not come from Middleton. It was probably written by Rowley. Some one says that Rowley was a third rate dramatist. To what class then must Middleton be relegated. April 1878

(Middleton, IV, 300) *The Changeling* [compare (Di, IV, 323)]

There is much movement in this play and there are scenes of interest. But it is so confused and inconsequent that the reader can too readily perceive the quick unnatural way in which the dramatists of James I looked into the plots which fell in their way. There is, however, more good work in this play than ever came from Middleton's hands. 20 April 1878

(Middleton, IV, 412) *A Game at Chess*

I have found that it was impossible to read this piece. There is a certain interest in the allusions to the religious feuds of the time; and the language in which these are described is sometimes good; — the abominations of the Papacy are well put forth; — but the dramatic form with the personages of the pawns &c, is so unreal, and so antipathetic to dramatic effect, that this piece is to me so dull as to be unreadable. 4 April 1877

[In Halliwell (p. 106) Trollope says: "Read in part but I could not get to the end April 4 1877"]

(Middleton, IV, 509-10) *Any Thing for a Quiet Life*

This play is readable; which is more than can be said of some of Middleton; and the character of Mrs. Knaverby, when she refuses to become a w——— at her husband's order is well, and in one or two lines, finely portrayed. But all the other characters are vapid and meaningless bad or good as the special scene may require. 9 April 1877

(Middleton, IV, 635) *Women Beware Women* [compare (Di, V, 127)]

The execution of the 3 first acts of this play is so good as to make the critic feel that Middleton, had he given himself fair chance by continued labour, might have excelled all the Elizabethan dramatists except Shakespeare. But the plot is so detestable, there not being a single part which is not abhorrent to the reader, that the same critic is driven to acknowledge that, with all his power of language, the author could never have become a great poet.

That Bianca and Livia should have been abominable one could have endured, had not Isabella have [sic] been equally bad. Her conscience was soon made easy when she was brought to think that her paramour was not Guard. her uncle.

The execution of the last portion of the play is as bad as the plot.

But it has to be acknowledged that there is wonderful work in the first three acts. 8 October 1876

(Middleton, V, 131) *No Wit, No Help Like a Woman's*

This is a bad play all round; — bad in language, bad in character, and bad in plot. And yet there is a certain activity about it that may have made it attractive on the stage to an audience devoid of all taste. The people with whom the reader is intended to sympathise are all bad; — and then there is not a single scene that is not badly told [?]. 10 March 1877

Otway, Thomas. *The Works of Thomas Otway.* 2 vols. London: J. Tonson, 1712.

(Otway, I, 208) *The Cheats of Scapin*

Utter trash. In poorness of subject Moliere is surpassed without any of the wit or polish or taste of Moliere. 12 September 1870 NO NOTES IN SECOND VOLUME

Peele, George. *The Works of George Peele.* Notes by Rev. Alexander Dyce. 2 vols. London: William Pickering, 1828.

(Peele, I, 67-68) *The Arraignment of Paris*

This is a most delightful piece of poetry and fairly merits the praise which on its behalf was given to the author by Nash, when he called Peele 'the chief supporter of pleasance now living, the Atlas of poetry,' and 'primus verborum artifex'* [pioneer craftsman of words]. There is a naive domestic familiar sweetness running through the play which quite justifies the description — It must be remembered that it was written before Midsummer Night's Dream, and that the compliment to Elizabeth which comes on the reader so unexpectedly on the solving of the plot of the play, probably gave rise to, certainly was not caused by, that excellent passage "That very time I saw, but then couldn't yet" — &c.

I cannot at all understand the preference given to David and Bethsabe. Dyce quotes Campbell's eulogy of that piece, and leaves us to imply that he agrees with it. The more that I read the less I am inclined to agree with much of the criticism on the English drama which I find from the pen of the best critical editors. 28 November 1878

[*Dyce quotes Nash in the introduction (p. xiii): ". . . I dare commend him unto all that know him, as the chiefe supporter of pleasance now living, the Atlas of poetrie, and primus verborum Artifex."]

(Peele, I, 200) *Edward I* [compare (Do, XI, 97)]

This is a marvellous example of such a play as could give delight in the earlier part of Queen Elizabeths reign. It is an abridgement of the incidents of a long reign, as is chiefly remarkable for the boldness with which the author could press on from one historical detail to another, without a pause. There is not much poetry in it, — but still there is some; and a somewhat grand idea of the feeling of a King and Queen. The real historical ignorance of the author is shewn by the introduction of all the horrors contained in the mythical ballad on Queen Eleanor [sic] no doubt the other incidents were taken from equally popular sources. 20 November 1878

(Peele, I, 248) *The Old Wives Tale*

An amusing and very wonderful farce, — giving an excellent instance of the differences between the dramatic literature of the Tudor and post-Tudor times. Milton no doubt got his Comus from Peele — from whence did Peele get his organisation of a plot? How pinchbeck will turn to gold in the hands of a great workman! The breaking away of Huanebango into the exclamations, p. 234 — taking up the lines no doubt then current of a poet of the time, is excessively droll — and what lines they are —

> "Oh that I might, but I may not! Woe to my
>   destiny therefore!
> "Kiss that I clasp, but I cannot; tell me,
>   my destiny, wherefore!"

What do we have in burlesque so good in these days. 24 November 1878

(Peele, I, flyleaf) *David and Bethsabe*

I find it impossible to understand praises lavished on this last piece, David & Bethsabe, in which all possible faults of composition seem to be combined. There is no character that demands or obtains sympathy. David is revolting in every act described. The episode of Ammon and Thamar is revolting — & yet it is so told that Absalon revolts in slaying Ammon. Absalon disgusts us throughout, & yet there is no gratitude to Joab for slaying Absalon. Bethsabe has nothing to do, — but that her acquiescence in David's wickedness, & the murder of her husband is still revolting. The lines are often grandiloquent, but their grandiloquence is turgid & when the critic is most tempted by their sound to hope that there is poetry, he is deterred by the lack of continuous sense. 20 September 1867

Shakespeare, William. *The Works of Shakespeare*. Revised by Alexander Dyce, 2nd. ed. 9 vols. London: Chapman and Hall, 1866-67.

(Shakespeare, I, 236) *The Tempest*

A very pretty play; but hardly in my mind equal to the praise bestowed upon it. It is said by some that to no play did the poet give more care and polish. I cannot see this. In the character of Miranda, the only woman, the readers imagination has to make up much that is not expressed. The celebrated sleep scene consists but of a few words. 4 July 1871

(Shakespeare, I, 324) *The Two Gentlemen of Verona*

This is surely a very poor play. 4 July 1871

(Shakespeare, I, 417) *The Merry Wives of Windsor*

This comedy is generally abused. I like it hugely. The Falstaff here is to my mind infinitely superior to that of Henry IV. 8 July 1871.

(Shakespeare, I, 521-22) *Measure for Measure*

Perhaps no play of this author is more uneven than this either in language plot or taste. The idea of Isabella's interference for her brother and her feeling that his death would be infinitely preferable to her own chastelessness [?] is not only fine but very fit for the stage.

I'll to my brother.
Though he has fallen by prompture of the blood,
Yet hath he in him such a mine [sic] of honour,
That had he twenty heads to tender down
On twenty blocks, he'd yield them sooner up,
Before his sister should her body stoop
To such abhorred pollution.

and Claudio's quaking fear is very good

Ay—but to die. etc.

Nevertheless that which is bad, coarse, and ill-done overwhelms the greatness sadly.

There are many passages in Shakespeare, written in prose which seem to us to have been so prepared as skeletons for the verse, into which when opportunity offered they were to be turned. The scene between Isabella and the Duke Act III. Sc. i is one of these. I have not heard this suggested, but in many plays I have fancied that it must be so. July 1875

(Shakespeare, II, 54) *The Comedy of Errors*

I have found more humour in this comedy than I used to credit it with; — the language too is thoroughly Shakespearean. 25 July 1871

(Shakespeare, II, 145) *Much Ado About Nothing*

This, which is an admirable comedy for the stage, is but a poor play to read. 27 June 1871

(Shakespeare, II, 236) *Love's Labour's Lost*

There is much sweetness and much fun in Love's Labour's Lost, — with some fine touches of poetry. But it becomes tedious and the action is not seldom unintelligible. It is better adapted for acting than for reading. 15 July 1875

(Shakespeare, II, 323) *A Midsummer-Night's Dream*

I know nothing in poetry prettier than the two first acts of a Midsummer's [sic] Night's Dream. The whole of it is good, but it falls off in the last three acts. The rhymed verse certainly adds a prettiness to the play. 4 June 1871

(Shakespeare, II, 416) *The Merchant of Venice*

In addition to the grand stage incidents of Shylock this play has as much of the beauty of poetry as any written by Shakespeare. There is no better reading. 18 June 1875

(Shakespeare, III, 77-78) *As You Like It*

This, perhaps, is the prettiest comedy that ever was written in any language. It is like a fairy tale, perfect in grace and beauty, but without fairies. The poet has dared to throw all probabilities to the wind. Fathers do not know their own children under the thinnest disguise; nor lovers their own sweethearts. Villains become good men at a moments notice. Hearts are changed and given away at a word. Lions roar where no lions ever where [sic]. The nature of snakes is made anew. But for all this the thoughts and language are as true to life as in any work that ever came from a mans pen. As a pastoral, it beats all pastorals. As a love story it is most charming. For comedy nothing can equal Touchstone and Audrey. The play is equally good whether acted or read; — only that actors for such parts as Rosalind, Orlando, Jaques, and Touchstone can hardly be found. 19 July 1875

(Shakespeare, III, 179) *The Taming of the Shrew*

This is better for the stage than the closet. The language, however, has often the true ring of the poets spirit. The repartee, which in Shakespeare's plays is frequently unintelligible to me, and frequently so far-fetched as hardly to be witty, is, in this play, very far far [sic] fetched and very unintelligible. 22 July 1871

(Shakespeare, III, 286) *All's Well That Ends Well*

The plot of this play is distasteful, especially the repetition of the idea of the true wife being substituted for the girl who was to be seduced as told before, — and much better told in Measure for Measure. The character of Bertram is abominable. That Angelo should have become the happy husband of Mariana was disagreeable; — but the final reception of Bertram into general favour is much worse.

The plots of these comedies, — and of one or two others, such as Much Ado About Nothing, & Twelfth Night are fitted for tales such as those of Boccaccio than for plays.

Parolles, — and one or two morsels of fine poetry redeem this piece. 26 July 1871

(Shakespeare, III, 396) *Twelfth-Night or What You Will*

A very pretty comedy, full of sweet poetry & infinite wit. The character of Viola is most charming. 29 June 1871

(Shakespeare, III, 506) *The Winter's Tale*

I think there is no plot of Shakespeare's so faulty as that of the Winter's Tale. But there is hardly a sweeter character than that of Perdita. Pity that there is so little of it. 26 June 1871

(Shakespeare, IV, 100) *King John*

This, the first of the historical plays, contains certain passages which beat all the others in poetic diction. Much of this is put into the mouths of unexpected [?] characters, — because there is so much of it. See especially speeches by the Bastard, Louis, and Salisbury.

It is chiefly by the passages in regard to Arthur, the scenes with Hubert, and the lamentations of Constance that the play is known to the world of readers. And the Bastard is chiefly remembered by Austria's calf's skin. But the character of the Bastard, from first to last, and especially in the last two acts is very great.

There are in King John marvellous instances of Elizabethan conceits, most distasteful to our ears, — as when Constance thus addresses Death —

> Thou odoriferous stench; — sound rottenness!

Doubtless in Shakespeare's time this was accepted as a proper [?] paradox. 16 June 1871

(Shakespeare, IV, 182) *King Richard II*

A somewhat dull play, with many most exquisite lines in it, bearing the full richness of Shakespeare's hand, — as, for instance, the following

> "He fires the proud tops of the Eastern pines;"
> or again
> "Not all the waters in the rough rude sea
> "Can wash the balm from an anointed king."

The kings part is the finest and the mixture of the strength of arrogant royalty with the weakness of sensual humanity, — the joint man and king, — is very striking. 19 June 1871

(Shakespeare, IV, 288) *First Part of Henry IV*

See second part.

(Shakespeare, IV, 402) *Second Part of Henry IV*

The historical plays of Shakespeare are best known by the characters of Constance, Falstaff and Wolsey; and the fat knight is in truth their hero. No character Shakespeare has drawn is more popular, and consequently Henry IVth is one of the plays with which ordinary readers are well acquainted. I have read these two plays a score of times and have relished their fun. But surely there is too much of it. The vocabulary of abuse between Falstaff, Pointz, Bardolph and the Prince becomes almost nasty. The last scene of Act II. Part I, which is one of the longest in all these plays, is next door to being tedious; but it shows the confidence the poet had in the character of Falstaff. The finest bit of poetry in the two plays, — indeed the only very fine passage, — is that in which the Prince takes away the crown. 22 June 1871

(Shakespeare, IV, 508) *King Henry V*

The comedy of this play is for the most part poor. Even the time honoured parallel of Macedon and Monmouth has not much in it. The French part, — ie. that given in French, — is very poor indeed.

The king's soliloquy on the state of kings is very grand indeed. 22 June 1875

(Shakespeare, V, 82) *King Henry VI*

See end of Part III.

(Shakespeare, V, 197) *King Henry VI*

See end of Part III.

(Shakespeare, V, 320) *Third Part of King Henry VI*

I consider it to have been impossible that Shakespeare should have written these three pieces. In all his works, — even the English historical plays, there is a culminating point of interest. Some period or incident is seized on which to hang the narrative. There is none such in Henry VI. Then Shakespeare always excites sympathy. In these plays the reader can sympathise neither with York or Lancaster; — nor yet with Warwick. The men are all traitors and murderers except the king, — who is thoroughly ignoble. Margaret is Suffolk's whore. Ellinor [sic] is a sorceress. Again whole lines of Latin are quoted, which I think Shakespeare neither did or could have done. And lastly the tedium of the whole is like to nothing that Shakespeare ever did.

There is a large amount of equable and sonorous poetry in these plays for much of which, though it be never very fine, Shakespeare may be responsible; but if so this has been his addition to works of other writers which it has been worth while to arrange for the stage. 16 June 1875

(Shakespeare, V, 454;478) *King Richard III*

[p. 454] See end notes.
[p. 478] The action of this play is magnificent and perpetual, and the concentration of interest in the wickedness and ambition of one man complete. The scheme of the play is intelligible as the plot is one whole and is not frittered into bits, as in Henry VI. The poetry is grand and occasionally majestic. But there is no single character with whom to sympathise. Anne and Elizabeth are satires on the sex, and the two old women are good only at cursing. 10 June 1871

(Shakespeare, V, 572; 595) *King Henry VIII*

[p. 572] See end of notes.
[p. 595] This is, I think, the finest of the historical pieces, possessing higher dramatic interest than any of the others.
The scope of history taken in these plays, from Richard II downwards almost to the authors days, giving in a poetical form the history of England with much historical truth, is most wonderful. The audacity of the quick movement through fleeting years astonishes the reader. The progress is made as though the poet felt no difficulty in it, though every writer knows how hard it is to tell of the sudden flight of years without some bold or inartistic explanation.
The heartfelt honour in which Shakespeare held kingship is shewn in all these plays; as in so many others; — noticeably in Hamlet by the well-worn line, and again in Winter's Tale.

> "If I could find example
> "Of thousands that had struck anointed kings
> "And flowers hid after, I'd not do it. But since
> "Nor brass, nor stone, nor parchment bears not one,
> "Let villainy itself forswear it."

How as to the striking of Richard II by Henry IV. 30 June 1871

(Shakespeare, VI, 100; 130) *Troilus and Cressida*

[p. 100] See end of notes.
[p. 130] I do not care much for this play — Cressida is too abominable. And the Pagan treatment of women as we may imagine it to have existed

118

at Troy is too much mingled with the feelings of Shakespeare's day. The familiarity of diction teaches us to regard Lord Pandarus as an uncle of Elizabeth's time.

The Grecian generals are long and dull. — "Where's then the saucy boat." is very fine. Thersites and Ajax do not please me at all — "Yon men will never tarry," is exquisitely sweet. 23 June 1871

(Shakespeare, VI, 238) *Coriolanus*

The conception of the character of Coriolanus is magnificently grand; but the play itself, as it is told, is often heavy, — especially in the first three acts. The expression too is often obscene, — almost as much so as in Cymbeline — Nevertheless Coriolanus, because of the greatness of the great Roman's character, is a very great play. 27 June 1871

(Shakespeare, VI, 354) *Titus Andronicus*

I cannot believe that Shakespeare wrote this play. It contains some grand lines; but it is the grandeur of Fletcher or of Ford, rather than of Shakespeare. There is a disgusting horror in the whole piece which was to Ford's taste, — and to that of Marlowe; but not to that of Shakespeare.

Shakespeare often quotes certain Latin phrases, which he had probably picked up about the theatres; but, as I think, never does quote Latin lines in a manner to shew that he knows the work of this or that poet. "Integer vitae, scelerisque purus" is, I think, unlike Shakespeare. Shakespeare makes many anachronisms but never so bad as that of talking of popish tricks in Pagan Rome. 17 July 1871

(Shakespeare, VI, 474) *Romeo and Juliet*

There are exquisite passages in this play, — passages in which the poetry of passionate love is expressed with language more rapturous than any other that I know; but in other respects the piece seems hardly to me to warrant its great reputation. The tragedy in the winding up of its plot becomes bloodthirsty to confusion, — as indeed does that of Hamlet. 7 July 1871

(Shakespeare, VI, 576) *Timon of Athens*

This play is surely unnatural in its plot to such a degree as to prevent sympathy. Timon himself is so unjust in his prosperity, that one almost feels that his adversity serves him right. The finest lines in the play are in Timon's speeches to Apemantius and to the robbers in Act. IV sc. iii. 7 July 1871

(Shakespeare, VI, 687) *Julius Caesar*

In this play is perhaps the finest character ever drawn by Shakespeare. No where is greater skill in delineation and a closer knowledge of human nature shewn than in Brutus. The honesty of the man, and the ill adaptation of the man's honesty to political exigencies and the purposes of conspiracy would hardly seem to be a subject for poetry; but the poetry is as grand as the character-painting is minute.

Antony's last speech is a magnificent description of Brutus-

> "This was the noblest Roman of them all
> x x x x x x x x x x x
> "Nature might stand up; And say to all the
> world There was a man."

22 July 1871

(Shakespeare, VII, 98) *Macbeth*

I regard Macbeth as being on the whole the finest play of Shakespeare. The plot is better than that of any of the other tragedies, and the pathos better sustained to the end. The language is never for a moment neglected, and the parts are all maintained with a proportionate excellence. The character of Duncan is exquisite, that of Banquo well carried through, and those of the attendant lords all good in subordination. Those of Macbeth and his wife are appalling in the gradual exercise of the horror of their crimes. In the mouth of Lady Macbeth even the rhyme of the two concluding lines is grand.

> "Which shall to all our days and nights to come
> Give solely sovereign sway and masterdom."

The sweetness is often ravishing, — as with Banquo

> "Buttress, nor coign of vantage, but this bird
> "Hath made her pendent bed and procreant cradle"

No words can be happier; — not even the soldier's, "And fortune on his damned quarrel smiling / Shewed like a rebel's whore."

The fault of the play is in the characters of Malcolm and Donaldbain [sic]. The 3rd scene of act IV in which Malcolm tries the temper of Macduff is absurd and dull; — but what is one such scene in such a play?

28 July 1871

[In the Isaac Reed (21 vol.) edition of Shakespeare Trollope makes a note on one of the footnotes in *Macbeth*. In Act I.sc.vii, vol. X, pp. 77-80, we find Macbeth's famous lines with a footnote number:

If it were done, when 'tis done, then 'twere well
It were done quickly: If the assassination
Could trammel up the consequence, and catch,
With his surcease, success;[8]

Footnote 8 offers Johnson's, Steevens', and then M. Mason's comments on these lines. It is Mason's comment that Trollope responds to. Mason says: "The personal pronouns are so frequently used by Shakespeare, instead of the impersonal, that no amendment would be necessary in this passage, even if it were certain that the pronoun *his* refers to *assassination*, which seems to be the opinion of Johnson and Steevens; but I think it more probable that it refers to *Duncan*; and that by his surcease Macbeth means *Duncan's* death, which was the object of his contemplation." Beside this note Trollope writes "yes" and then, "I would read the meaning of these lines as: — If Duncan's assassination could be hidden in its consequences, that the matter should end there & success follow; if this blow might be the last I should live to strike on earth, — I'd hazard the life to me." (p. 79)]

(Shakespeare, VII, 211) *Hamlet*

Of this, which as far as my reading and judgement go, is the greatest work of man, it is impossible to speak correctly in a criticism so abridged as this must be. It is remarkable that that [sic] in a play where all else is perfect, the last scene should be so incongruous and so little affecting. The madness of Hamlet, so called, I take to be double in its nature. That he affected madness is, I think certain, but he is also intended to be drawn as afflicted with a certain melancholy, which unmans him and accounts for his cruelty to Ophelia.

The interest of the play is almost confined to one character — Ophelia, pretty as she is, has but an indifferent part. Polonius is well known because of his well-worn wisdom, and as being an easy part. Next to Hamlet the King has the best of it. 3 May 1871

The above I think to be in the main correct; but Shakespeare has been indifferent as to the conduct of all of his personages, and has contented himself in seeking excellence in the finish of his thought and in the choice language in which he expresses it. The last scene of the play is bad but the piece taken as a whole has no equal in any langauge. Warburton, Johnson, Steevens and Malone* have overloaded it with criticism, none of which is good. December 1880

[*Trollope is here referring to the 21 volume edition of Shakespeare (owned now by the Folger Library, see Appendix C) that gives the collected criticism of these men.]

(Shakespeare, VII, 346) *King Lear*

There is nothing, perhaps, in the whole range of poetry to exceed the finest passages of Lear, and I know no character in which so grand a passion is displayed. Edgar is very excellent, and shews infinite skill in the manner in which the pretended Tom of Bedlam is enabled, without departing from his assumed character to speak not a word that is not pregnant with wit, pathos, or philosophy. The fool is certainly the best of Shakespeare's fools.

The play falls off from Othello in this; — that Edmund, the villain, is but a poor creature as compared with Iago. In villainy the one is almost the counterpart of the other; — but, as characters in a piece, Edmund lacks all that wondrous skill in mischief combined with wit, which makes Iago almost as great a part as Othello.

The end of Lear is weak and unnecessarily bloody, — as is that of Hamlet. 18 July 1871

(Shakespeare, VII, 470) *Othello*

The plot, performance, and language of this play are alike perfect. It is assuredly one of the grandest works of human genius. The manipulation of the character of Iago has perhaps in it as much of the cleverness of a plot, — as many foreseen consequences of each act and word, as any-thing in fiction, either in prose or poetry. 30 June 1871

(Shakespeare, VII, 598) *Antony and Cleopatra*

This I think to be one of Shakespeare's finest plays. The two characters are admirably carried out, and the language throughout is grand and poetic. With the exception of Cleopatra's detestable attempt to screen her wealth from Octavius, all the incidents are worthy of the general action. How infinitely finer is the character of the bad Antony than that of Coriolanus who is intended to be good! The same may be said of Cleopatra as compared with Volumnia and Virgilia. 9 July 1871

(Shakespeare, VII, 735) *Cymbeline*

The part of Imogen and the one well known speech by Iachimo in Imogen's chamber have made this play famous among the great works of the poet. In other respects it is tedious, — not without poetic passages; — but often intricate as well as tedious, and also obscene. Some of the poets fail utterly; — as those of Posthumus and Cloten. The Queen is altogether uninteresting; and Cymbeline lacks that majestic walk with which Shakespeare almost always endows majesty.

Let any reader take Hamlet first, and then Cymbeline, and calculate what amount of matter he has got from the one, and from the other!!

But Imogen redeems the play. She is the sweetest wife in all poetry. 23 July 1871

(Shakespeare, VIII, 74) *Pericles*

I cannot believe that Shakespeare wrote this play. There is to my ears nothing in it of his manner, and to my understanding none of his genius. The easy boldness with which a long period of time is dealt with and the rapidity of startling incidents give assurance that this is the work of a practical playwright; — but the play itself is very bad. I never read it before. 1 July 1871

(Shakespeare, VIII, 210) *Two Noble Kinsmen*

See remarks on the play in Beaumont and Fletcher's works. It contains some very fine work from Shakespeare's hands. 8 October 1874

[The rest of vol. VIII has poetry and no ms. notes and vol. IX is a glossary and has no notes.]

Shirley, James. *The Dramatic Works and Poems.* Notes by W. Gifford and Rev. Alexander Dyce. 6 vols. London: J. Murray, 1833.

(Shirley, I, 362) *The Witty Fair One*

A very poor play indeed, — alluring only by its indecency, for, what would be wit is far-fetched and heavy. 14 May 1874

(Shirley, I, 450-51) *The Wedding*

[several passages marked by lines throughout the play] This play has passages in it so fine, — see the three first acts; and others so poor, — see the two last, as to make one wonder whether the whole piece be by the one author. But the better parts are so good as to force from the critic a measure [?] of the very highest praise. They have a flavour of all the poetry of Fletcher. The play swells [?] to all the mediocrity even combined [?] by Dekker or Heywood. But in truth we do not know who wrote these Stuart plays. One man and another worked together, and the audience seemed to have taken the wheat and the chaff and hardly to have noted the difference. 11 October 1880

(Shirley, II, 93-94) *The Grateful Servant*

As plays went at the time this was an admirable play, — infinitely superior to half of those given in this collection, Dodsley's and others, and much better than very many of Fletchers. The language is frequently very fine, sometimes quite worthy of Shakespeare almost at his best.

> Thou shouldst have watched her cheek then blush
> There as had been guilt indeed. A feeble answer, with
> half a smile, had been an argument she had been lost.

And this excellence of language is carried throughout, — even into the prose, — which toward the last act shows, as was so common, that the author lacked the perseverance to turn it into verse.

But the plot, or plots, is abominable as far as sympathy goes, though one can perceive that they admitted of fine acting. The idea that it was a good thing to give up to another a lady who was truly loving and truly loved, because that other was a duke is a wretched thought. The idea, too, of rescuing Lodwick from vice by the proposed offer to him of the old tutor's young wife, the offer being made jointly in most libidinous language by both husband & wife, is detestable, and could only have been possible while men took women's parts—Astellas continued regard for Lodwick is almost equally bad— But all these faults were the faults of the taste of the age rather than of the poet. 12 May 1874

(Shirley, II, 188) *The Traitor*

This is an admirable tragedy; or rather a tragedy with admirable passages. It is well worth the reading as being full of poetry. Amidea is twice tempted by the brother. The first temptation is by far the finer. I observe that in most of these plays the spirit or energy of the poet hardly carries him through equably to the end. The character of the Duke is certainly weaker and the second plot concerning Oriana is very weak and almost unintelligible. The play however should certainly be named as one of the finest of the age. 3 December 1880

(Shirley, III, 91) *The Ball* [compare (B, I, iv)]

An amusing play, without very much either of character or of wit. One can understand that it would act well. Shirley seems always to have written expressly for the actor. 16 May 1874
    See also Baldwins [sic] collection

(Shirley, III, 181) *The Young Admiral*

The three first acts of this are very good, full of poetry, and the plot well carried through, — but it falls off tremendously in the two last acts, so as

124

to run into numberless absurdities. The "off with his head"* on the part
of one of the king seems to have given rise to later caricatures.

But the character of Vittori is excellently well sustained till the poet
becomes hurried in his work. 4 October 1880

[* *Was* Trollope thinking of Lewis Carroll's *Alice* (1865)?]

(Shirley, III, 278) *The Gamester*

The plot of Wilding and his wife Will Hazard and Penelope is amusing,
and the language always readable, — sometimes well chosen. What
becomes of Shirley's "Chaste Muse" the reader must ask. It is after all
only said to "comparatively chaste," anything less chaste than the telling
of the story I cannot imagine. The second plot as to Delamore & Leonora
is passed over and all but forgotten. He had found his plots and then
hurried on to the riches of his drama, — as they all did. 1 November 1880
Why should it have been called The Gamester? Shirley began with the
idea of a gambling set, and then forgot to write up to it.

(Shirley, III, 365) *The Example*

This is an absurd play in which one knows not with whom to sympathise,
or where to find the points at which to laugh and be amused, and the
language is generally prose cut down with a measuring rod to blank
verse. See the speech of Lord FitzA[varice] Act V. 2 which I have marked.*
But atonement is made by the happy expression of "Confident's" flattery.
One would think that this special character had been written by some
greater dramatist. 15 February 1881

[*The passage begins (p. 358), "To satisfy my wantonness; but found/ An innocence so rich in
her, as may/ Alone excuse"]

(Shirley, IV, 100) *The Lady of Pleasure*

This is on the whole a poor play, with a great deal of the attempted
allurement which comes from gross obscenity. The modest women are
made to say immodest words. There are a few passages which are near to
fine poetry, but do not quite touch it, — as when act V. scene i the lord
says

> "And violets stoop to have us tread upon 'em"

But even this is destroyed by such a phrase as Repuring the air! 6
February 1881

Appendix A
ALPHABETICAL LIST OF
PLAYWRIGHTS AND THEIR PLAYS

See KEY TO THE TEXT for an explanation of abbreviations, spelling of titles, and attribution of authorship. An asterisk is used here to indicate that a play is listed under more than one playwright.

Playwright	Play	Edition
B.,R.	*Appius and Virginia*	Do, XII, 377
BALE	*God's Promises*	Do, I, 42
BARRY	*Ram-Alley or Merry Tricks*	Do, V, 459-60
BEAUMONT &	*Beggar's Bush*	BF, IX, 104
FLETCHER	*The Bloody Brother*	BF, X, 467-68
	or Rollo, Duke of Normandy	
	Bonduca	BF, V, 102
	The Captain	BF, III, 327-28
	The Chances	BF, VII, 303
	The Coxcomb	BF, III, 215
	Cupid's Revenge	BF, II, 449
	The Custom of the Country	BF, IV, 494
	The Double Marriage	BF, VI, 414
	The Elder Brother	BF, X, 292
	The Fair Maid of the Inn	BF, X, 105
	The Faithful Friends	BF, IV, 300-01
	The Faithful Shepherdess	BF, II, 121
	The False One	BF, VI, 306-07
	Four Plays in One	BF, II, 570
	The Honest Man's Fortune	BF, III, 452
	The Humorous Lieutenant	BF, VI, 538-40
	The Island Princess	BF, VII, 513
	A King and No King	BF, II, 347
	The Knight of the Burning Pestle	BF, II, 229
	The Knight of Malta	BF, V, 206-07
	The Laws of Candy	BF, V, 392
	The Little French Lawyer	BF, III, 563
	Love's Cure	BF, IX, 194-95
	Love's Pilgrimage	BF, XI, 323
	The Lovers' Progress	BF, XI, 118
	The Loyal Subject	BF, VI, 113
	The Mad Lover	BF, VI, 212-13
	The Maid in the Mill	BF, IX, 294
	The Maid's Tragedy	BF, I, 425
	Monsieur Thomas	BF, VII, 411

	Honest Whore, Pt. Two	De, II, 183; cr. Do, III, 425; cr. Mi, III, 244
	The King's Entertainment Through the City of London	De, I, 326
	Old Fortunatus	De, I, 174; Di, III, 219
	The Roaring Girl or Moll Cut-Purse	Mi, II, 559; Do, VI, 106; cr. De, III, 232
	The Sun's Darling	F, III, 169; cr. De, IV, 344
	The Untrussing of the Humorous Poet	De, I, 264
	The Virgin Martyr	Mas, I, 121; cr. De, IV, 91
	The Witch of Edmonton	F, III, 271; cr. De, IV, 427
	The Wonder of a Kingdom	De, IV, 286; Di, III, 98
DIGBY	Elvira	Do, XII, 212
EDWARDS	Damon and Pithias	Do, I, 260
FISHER [?]	The True Trojans	Do, VII, 456-57
FORD	The Broken Heart	F, I, 319
	The Fancies Chaste and Noble	F, II, 321
	The Lady's Trial	F, III, 98
	Love's Sacrifice	F, II, 108
	The Lover's Melancholy	F, I, 105
	Perkin Warbeck	F, II, 217
	The Sun's Darling	F, III, 169; cr. De, IV, 344
	'Tis Pity She's a Whore	F, I, 208
	The Witch of Edmonton	F, III, 271; cr. De, IV, 427
GASCOIGNE & KENWELMERSHE	Jocasta	C, I, 260
GLAPTHORNE	Albertus Wallenstein	B, II, x
	The Lady's Privilege	B, II, 78-79
GREENE	Friar Bacon and Friar Bungay	G, I, 214; Do, VIII, 240
[?]	George a Greene, The Pinner of Wakefield	G, II, 205; Do, III, 48
	James the Fourth	G, II, 128, 152
	Orlando Furioso	G, I, 53
HABINGTON	The Queen of Arragon	Do, IX, 410
HEYWOOD, JOHN	The Four P's	Do, I, 102
	The Pardoner and the Frere	C, I, 89
HEYWOOD, TH.	The Brazen Age	H, III, 256
	A Challenge for Beauty	H, V, 78; Di, VI, 424

	The English Traveller	H, IV, 95; Di, VI, 218
[?]	*The Faire Maid of the Exchange*	H, II, 87
	The Fair Maid of the West or A Girl Worth Gold	H, II, 332
	The Fair Maid, Pt. Two	H, II, 423
	The Four Prentices of London	H, II, 254; cr. Do, VI, 486
	The Golden Age	H, III, 79
	The Iron Age, Pt. One	H, III, 345
	The Iron Age, Pt. Two	H, III, 431-32
	King Edward the Fourth	H, I, 90
	King Edward the Fourth, II	H, I, 187
	Love's Mistress	B, II, xxiv; H, V, 160
	A Mayden-head Well Lost	H, IV, 164
	The Rape of Lucrece	B, I, iv; H, V, 257
	The Royal King and Loyal Subject	H, VI, 83; Di, VI, 321
	The Silver Age	H, III, 164
	The Wise-woman of Hogsdon	H, V, 353
	The Witches of Lancashire	H, IV, 260
	A Woman Killed with Kindness	H, II, 157; cr. Do, VII, 289
[?]	*If You Know Not Me, You Know Nobody or The Troubles of Queen Eliza*	H, I, 247
[?]	*If You Know Not Me, Pt. Two*	H, I, 344
JONSON	*The Alchemist*	J, IV, 181-83
	Bartholomew Fair	J, IV, 510
	The Case is Altered	J, VI, 396-97
	Catiline	J, IV, 336
	Cynthia's Revels	J, II, 362
	The Devil is an Ass	J, V, 148-49
	*Eastward Hoe	Do, IV, 279; Mars, III, 101-02
	Every Man in His Humour	J, I, 150-51
	Every Man Out of His Humour	J, II, 197
	The Magnetic Lady	J, VI, 118
	The New Inn	J, V, 414
	Poetaster	J, II, 470, 510, 523-24
	The Sad Shepherd	J, VI, 288
	The Satyr	J, VI, 455
	Sejanus	J, III, 152-53
	The Silent Woman	J, III, 482
	The Staple of News	J, V, 293-94
	A Tale of a Tub	J, VI, 226
	Volpone	J, III, 323-24

KILLEGREW	*The Parson's Wedding*	Do, XI, 585
KYD	*Cornelia*	Do, II, 303
[?]	*Jeronimo*	Do, III, 94
	The Spanish Tragedy	Do, III, 202
LODGE	*The Wounds of Civil War*	Do, VIII, 10
LYLY	*Alexander and Campaspe*	Do, II, 150
	Endymion	Di, II, 97
	Midas: A Comedy	Di, I, 371
	Mother Bombie	Di, I, 287
MACHIN &	*The Dumb Knight*	Do, IV, 451-52
MARKHAM		
MARLOWE	*Dido, Queen of Carthage*	B, II, xiv
	Edward II	Mar, II, 290;
		cr. Do, II, 404
	The Jew of Malta	Mar, I, 349;
		cr. Do, VIII, 327
	Lust's Dominion	Di, I, 195
	The Massacre at Paris	Mar, II, 359
	Tamburlaine the Great, Pt.II	Mar, I, 226
	The Tragedy of Doctor Faustus	Mar, II, 84;
		Di, I, 88
MARMION	*The Antiquary*	Do, X, 96
MARSTON	*Antonio's Revenge*	Mars, I, 144
	The Dutch Courtezan	Mars, II, 192
	*Eastward Hoe	Mars, III, 101-02;
		Do, IV, 279
	History of Antonio and Mellida	Mars, I, 68-69
		Di, II, 191
	The Malcontent	Mars, II, 292;
		cr. Do, IV, 96
	Parasitaster or The Fawn	Mars, II, 106;
		Di, II, 407
	The Tragedie of Sophonisba	Mars, I, 215
	What You Will	Mars, I, 218;
		Di, II, 290
MASSINGER	*The Bashful Lover*	Mas, IV, 453
	The Bondman	Mas, II, 117
	The City Madam	Mas, IV, 116
	The Duke of Milan	Mas, I, 343-44
	The Emperor of the East	Mas, III, 344-45
	The Fatal Dowry	Mas, III, 474-75
	The Great Duke of Florence	Mas, II, 520
	The Guardian	Mas, IV, 232
	The Maid of Honour	Mas, III, 107
	A New Way to Pay Old Debts	Mas, III, 590
	*The Old Law	Mas, IV, 573; 584
		cr. Mi, I, 120
	The Parliament of Love	Mas, II, 322
	The Picture	Mas, III, 231-32

	The Renegado	Mas, II, 231
	The Roman Actor	Mas, II, 420-21
	The Unnatural Combat	Mas, I, 230
	A Very Woman	Mas, IV, 343
	* The Virgin-Martyr	Mas, I, 121;
		cr. De, IV, 91
MAY	*The Heir*	Do, VIII, 162
	The Old Couple	Do, X, 447
MAYNE	*The City-Match*	Do, IX, 328
MIDDLETON	*Blurt, Master Constable*	Mi, I, 308-09
	* The Changeling	Mi, IV, 300;
		Di, IV, 323
	A Chaste Maid in Cheapside	Mi, IV, 88
	A Fair Quarrel	Mi, III, 549
	The Family of Love	Mi, II, 209
	A Game at Chess	Mi, IV, 412
	* The Honest Whore	De, II, 91;
		cr. Mi, III, 122;
		cr. Di, II,I, 322
	* Honest Whore, Pt. Two	De, II, 183;
		cr. Mi, III, 122;
		cr. Do, III, 425
	* A Mad World, My Masters	Mi, II, 422;
		cr. Do, V, 358
[?]	** The Mayor of Quinborough*	Mi, I, 222;
		Do, XI, 183
[?]	*Michaelmas Term*	Mi, I, 514
	More Dissemblers Besides Women	Mi, III, 645;
		Di, IV, 428-29
	No Wit, No Help Like a Woman's	Mi, V, 131
	* The Old Law	Mas, IV, 573; 584;
		cr. Mi, I, 120
[?]	*The Phoenix*	Mi, I, 409
	* The Roaring Girl	Mi, II, 559;
		Do, VI, 106;
		cr. De, III, 232
	* The Spanish Gipsy	Mi, IV, 202;
		Di, IV, 218
	* A Trick to Catch the Old One	Mi, II, 99;
		Di, V, 224
	* The Widow	BF, IV, 383;
		Do, XII, 295;
		Cr. Mi, III, 440
	The Witch	Mi, III, 335
	Women Beware Women	Mi, IV, 635
		Di, V, 127
	Your Five Gallants	Mi, II, 323
NABBES	*Microcosmus*	Do, IX, 137
NASH	*Summer's Last Will*	Do, IX, 79

131

OTWAY	The Cheats of Scapin	O, I, 208
PEELE	The Arraignment of Paris	P, I, 67-68
	David and Bethsabe	P, I, flyleaf
	Edward I	P, I, 200; Do, XI, 97
	The Old Wives Tale	P, I, 248
PRESTON	King Cambises	Ha, I, 317
RANDOLPH	The Muse's Looking Glass	Do, IX, 225
ROWLEY	*The Changeling	Mi, IV, 300; Di, IV, 323
	A Match at Midnight	Do, VII, 376
	A New Wonder: A Woman Never Vext	Di, V, 348
	*The Old Law	Mas, IV, 573; 584; cr. Mi, I, 120
	*The Spanish Gipsy	Mi, IV, 202; Di, IV, 218
	*The Thracian Wonder	Di, VI, 98
SACKVILLE & NORTON	Gorboduc or Ferrex and Porrex	Do, I, 173
SHAKESPEARE	All's Well that Ends Well	Sh, III, 286
	Antony and Cleopatra	Sh, VII, 598
	As You Like It	Sh, III, 77-78
	The Comedy of Errors	Sh, II, 54
	Coriolanus	Sh, VI, 238
	Cymbeline	Sh, VII, 735
	Hamlet	Sh, VII, 211
	Henry IV, Parts I & II	Sh, IV, 402
	Julius Caesar	Sh, VI, 687
	King Henry V	Sh, IV, 508
	King Henry VI, Parts I, II, III	Sh, V, 320
	King Henry VIII	Sh, V, 595
	King John	Sh, IV, 100
	King Lear	Sh, VII, 346
	King Richard II	Sh, IV, 182
	King Richard III	Sh, V, 478
	Love's Labour's Lost	Sh, II, 236
	Macbeth	Sh, VII, 98
	Measure for Measure	Sh, I, 521-22
	The Merchant of Venice	Sh, II, 416
	The Merry Wives of Windsor	Sh, I, 417
	A Midsummer-Night's Dream	Sh, II, 323
	Much Ado About Nothing	Sh, II, 145
	Othello	Sh, VII, 470
	Pericles	Sh, VIII, 74
	Romeo and Juliet	Sh, VI, 474
	The Taming of the Shrew	Sh, III, 179
	The Tempest	Sh, I, 236
	Timon of Athens	Sh, VI, 576
	Titus Andronicus	Sh, VI, 354
	Troilus and Cressida	Sh, VI, 130

	Twelfth-Night	Sh, III, 396
	The Two Gentlemen of Verona	Sh, I, 324
	* *Two Noble Kinsmen*	cr. Sh, VIII, 210; BF, XI, 437
	The Winter's Tale	Sh, III, 506
SHIRLEY	* *The Ball*	S, III, 91; B, I, iv
	The Example	S, III, 365
	The Gamester	S, III, 278
	The Grateful Servant	S, II, 93-94
	The Lady of Pleasure	S, IV, 100
	The Traitor	S, II, 188
	The Wedding	S, I, 450-51
	The Witty Fair One	S, I, 362
	The Young Admiral	S, III, 181
STILL [?]	*Gammer Gurton's Needle*	Do, II, 83; Ha, I, 242
SUCKLING	*The Goblins*	Do, X, 161
T., J.	*Grim the Collier of Croydon*	Do, XI, 258-59
TAILOR	*The Hog Hath Lost His Pearl*	Do, VI, 393
TOMKIS	*Albumazar*	Do, VII, 212
TOURNEUR [?]	*The Revenger's Tragedy*	Do, IV, 370
TUKE	*The Adventures of Five Hours*	Do, XII, 117
WEBSTER	*Appius and Virginia*	Di, V, 450;
	* *The Thracian Wonder*	Di, VI, 98
	The White Devil	Do, VI, 325-26
WEVER	*Lusty Juventus*	Ha, I, 163
WILKINS	*Inforced Marriage*	Do, V, 97
WILMOT	*Tancred and Gismunda*	Do, II, 234
WRIGHT	*Historia Histrionica*	Do, I, clxix
ANONYMOUS	*Candlemas Day*	Ha, I, 26
	Everyman	Ha, I, 68
	Hycke-Scorner	Ha, I, 111
	The Merry Devil	Do, V, 272
	New Custome	Do, I, 307-08
	The Second Maiden's Tragedy	B, I, iv-v
	Worlde and the Chylde	Do, XII, 336

CHRONOLOGICAL ORDER OF TROLLOPE'S DRAMA READING

The original schedule was first published in *Notes & Queries* 31 (Dec. 1984), 491-97. (Titles have been added here.) An asterisk indicates that a play has been read and commented on more than once. See KEY TO THE TEXT for an explanation of abbreviations, spelling, and attributions.

Date	Playwright	*Play*
26 Nov. 1866	BF	*The Maid's Tragedy*
20 Sept. 1867	Peele	*David and Bethsabe*
Oct.	Marston	*What You Will*
24 Nov.	Marlowe	*The Jew of Malta*
1 Dec.	Marl.	*Edward II*
2 Dec.	Marl.	*Doctor Faustus*
1 Jan. 1868	Marl.	*Sec. Pt. Tamburlaine the Great*
4 Mar. 1869	BF	*The Woman's Prize or the Tamer Tamed*
9 March	BF	*Knight of the Burning Pestle*
9 Jan. 1870	Marston	*The Dutch Courtezan*
30 April	Anon.	*The Second Maiden's Tragedy*
1 May	Cooke	*A Pleasant Conceited Comedy*
2 May	Chap. & Shir.	** The Ball*
3 May	Heywood	*The Rape of Lucrece*
30 May	Hey.	*Love's Mistress*
25 June	Glapthorne	*Albertus Wallenstein*
26 June	Marl. & Nash	*Dido, Queen of Carthage*
1 July	BF	*Rule a Wife and Have a Wife*
3 July	Glapthorne	*The Lady's Privilege*
7 July	Massinger	*A New Way to Pay Old Debts*
11 July 1870	Sackville & Norton	*Gorboduc or Ferrex and Porrex*
16 July	Still [?]	*Gammer Gurton's Needle*
17 July	Lyly	*Alexander and Campaspe*
23 July	Lyly	*Mother Bombie*
12 Sept.	Otway	*The Cheats of Scapin*
Jan. 1871	Ford	*'Tis Pity She's a Whore*
1 Jan.	Wilmot	*Tancred and Gismunda*
2 Jan.	Kyd [?]	*Jeronimo*
2 Jan.	Kyd	*Spanish Tragedy*
2 Jan.	Greene [?]	*Pinner of Wakefield*
4 Jan.	Greene	*Friar Bacon and Friar Bungay*
8 Jan.	Marston	*The Malcontent*
9 Jan.	Mars.	*Antonio and Mellida*

3 May	Shakespeare	*Hamlet*
4 June	Sh.	*A Midsummer-Night's Dream*
10 June	Sh.	*King Richard III*
16 June	Sh.	*King John*
19 June	Sh.	*King Richard II*
22 June	Sh.	*Henry IV, Parts I & II*
23 June	Sh.	*Troilus and Cressida*
26 June	Sh.	*The Winter's Tale*
27 June	Sh.	*Much Ado About Nothing*
27 June	Sh.	*Coriolanus*
29 June	Sh.	*Twelfth-Night*
30 June	Sh.	*King Henry VIII*
30 June	Sh.	*Othello*
1 July	Sh.	*Pericles*
4 July	Sh.	*The Tempest*
4 July	Sh.	*Two Gentlemen of Verona*
7 July	Sh.	*Romeo and Juliet*
7 July	Sh.	*Timon of Athens*
8 July	Sh.	*The Merry Wives of Windsor*
9 July	Sh.	*Antony and Cleopatra*
17 July	Sh.	*Titus Andronicus*
18 July	Sh.	*King Lear*
22 July	Sh.	*The Taming of the Shrew*
22 July	Sh.	*Julius Caesar*
23 July	Sh.	*Cymbeline*
25 July	Sh.	*The Comedy of Errors*
26 July	Sh.	*All's Well that Ends Well*
28 July	Sh.	*Macbeth*
7 June 1873	Jonson	*Eastward Hoe*
14 June	Chapman	*All Fools*
21 June	Brewer [?]	*Lingua*
6 July	Cook	*Green's Tu Quoque*
July	Tuke	*The Adventures of Five Hours*
7 Aug.	Middleton	*The Roaring Girl*
Oct.	Heywood	*The Pardoner and the Frere*
24 Oct.	Hey.	*The Four P's*
28 Oct.	Gascoigne & Kenwelmershe	*Jocasta*
16 Nov.	Dekker	*The Untrussing of the Humorous Poet*
22 Nov.	Dek.	*The Gentle Craft*
23 Nov.	Dek.	*Old Fortunatus*
Nov. 1873	Dek.	*The Honest Whore*
6 Dec.	Dek.	*Honest Whore, Pt. II*
11 Dec.	BF	*The Woman-Hater*
11 Dec.	BF	*The Faithful Shepherdess*
17 Dec.	BF	*The Scornful Lady*
20 Dec.	BF	*The Wild-Goose-Chase*
8 March	Marmion	*The Antiquary*
March	Bale	*God's Promises*

April	Edwards	*Damon and Pithias*
April	Webster	*The White Devil*
10 May	Tourneur [?]	*The Revenger's Tragedy*
12 May	Shirley	*The Grateful Servant*
14 May	Shir.	*The Witty Fair One*
16 May	Chap. & Shir.	**The Ball*
18 May	BF	*The Coxcomb*
25 May	BF	*The Custom of the Country*
29 May	Middleton	*Blurt, Master Constable*
3 June	Midd. [?]	*The Mayor of Quinborough*
8 June	BF	*A King and No King*
9 June	BF	*Bonduca*
11 June	BF	*Wit Without Money*
15 June	BF	*A Wife for a Month*
15 June	BF	*The Noble Gentleman*
17 June	BF	*Cupid's Revenge*
19 June	BF	*The Queen of Corinth*
22 June 1874	BF	*The Humorous Lieutenant*
24 June	Marston	*Antonio's Revenge*
27 June	BF	*Beggar's Bush*
3 July	BF	*The Elder Brother*
4 July	BF	*The Captain*
11 July	BF	*The Chances*
18 July	BF	*The Double Marriage*
July	BF	*The Prophetess*
16 Sept.	BF	*Monsieur Thomas*
18 Sept.	BF	*The Fair Maid of the Inn*
26 Sept.	BF	*Valentinian*
27 Sept.	BF	*Four Plays in One*
29 Sept.	BF	*The Nice Valour*
8 Oct.	BF	*Two Noble Kinsmen*
10 Oct.	BF	*Lover's Progress*
13 Oct.	BF	*The Mad Lover*
16 Oct.	BF	*The Spanish Curate*
23 Oct.	BF	*Women Pleased*
Oct.	BF	*The Honest Man's Fortune*
Oct.	BF	*The Loyal Subject*
Oct.	BF	*The Bloody Brother*
1 Nov.	BF	*The Laws of Candy*
24 Nov.	BF	*The Maid in the Mill*
30 Nov.	BF	*The Widow*
Nov.	BF	*The Little French Lawyer*
Nov.	BF	*Wit and Several Weapons*
Nov.	BF	*The Faithful Friends*
Nov.	BF	*The Island Princess*
Nov. 1874	BF	*Love's Cure*
8 Dec.	BF	*The Knight of Malta*
16 Dec.	BF	*The Pilgrim*
25 Dec.	BF	*The Night Walker or The Little Thief*
27 Dec.	BF	*Love's Pilgrimage*

136

Dec.	BF	*The False One*
Dec.	BF	*The Sea-Voyage*
Jan. 1875	Ford	*The Sun's Darling*
Jan.	Ford	*The Witch of Edmonton*
Jan.	Heywood	*The Four Prentices*
Jan.	Ford	*The Lover's Melancholy*
Jan.	Ford	*Perkin Warbeck*
Jan.	Heywood	*First Pt. Edward the Fourth*
Jan.	Hey.	*Sec. Pt. Edward the Fourth*
Jan.	Hey. [?]	*If you Know Not Me*
Jan.	Hey. [?]	*Sec. Pt. If You Know Not Me*
Jan.	Hey. [?]	*Faire Maide of the Exchange*
31 Jan.	Ford	*The Broken Heart*
28 Feb.	Ford	*The Fancies Chaste and Noble*
16 June	Shakespeare	*King Henry VI, Pts. I, II, III*
22 June	Sh.	*King Henry V*
15 July	Sh.	*Love's Labour's Lost*
19 July	Sh.	*As You Like It*
July	Sh.	*Measure for Measure*
Nov.	Jonson	*Sejanus
Dec.	Jon.	*Every Man in His Humour
Dec.	Jon.	*Every Man Out of His Humour*
Dec.	Jon.	*Poetaster
Xmas day	Jon.	*Cynthia's Revels*
26 Dec.	Jon.	*Volpone or the Fox
Jan. 1876	Jon.	*The Alchemist
Jan.	Jon.	*The Silent Woman*
Jan. 1876	Jon.	*Catiline*
25 Feb.	Jon.	*The Satyr*
27 Feb.	Jon.	*The Case is Altered*
Feb.	Jon.	*Bartholomew Fair*
March	Jon.	*The Devil is an Ass*
March	Jon.	*The Staple of News*
March	Massinger	*The Fatal Dowry*
1 April	Mass.	*The Guardian*
21 April	Mass.	*The Renegado*
22 April	Mass.	*The City Madam*
28 April	Mass.	*The Maid of Honour*
30 April	Mass.	*The Parliament of Love*
April	Mass.	*The Virgin-Martyr*
April	Mass.	*The Unnatural Combat*
April	Mass.	*The Bondman*
5 May	Jonson	*The Magnetic Lady*
May	Jon.	*The New Inn*
1 June	Jon.	*A Tale of a Tub*
2 June	Jon.	*The Sad Shepherd*
4 June	Marlowe	*The Massacre at Paris*
18 June	Machin & Markham	*The Dumb Knight*
24 June	Mass.	*The Picture*

June	Greene	*Orlando Furioso*
7 July	Ford	*The Lady's Trial*
8 July	Mass.	** The Old Law*
15 July	Mass.	*The Great Duke of Florence*
29 July	Mass.	*The Duke of Milan*
29 July	Mass.	*The Roman Actor*
1 Aug.	Mass.	*The Emperor of the East*
6 Aug.	Mass.	*A Very Woman*
6 Aug.	Mass.	*The Bashful Lover*
8 Oct.	Midd.	*Women Beware Women*
15 Jan. 1877	Midd.	*A Trick to Catch the Old One*
Jan.	Midd.	*The Witch*
17 Feb.	Midd. [?]	*The Phoenix*
4 March	Midd.	*The Family of Love*
10 March	Midd.	*No Wit, No Help Like a Woman's*
31 March	Midd.	*A Chaste Maid in Cheapside*
4 April	Midd.	*A Game at Chess*
9 April	Midd.	*Anything for a Quiet Life*
27 April	Midd.	*More Dissemblers Besides Women*
6 Feb. 1878	Midd. [?]	*Michaelmas Term*
24 March	Midd.	*Your Five Gallants*
31 March	Midd.	*A Fair Quarrel*
20 April	Midd. & Row.	*The Changeling*
23 April	Midd.	*A Mad World, My Masters*
April	Midd. & Row.	*The Spanish Gipsy*
6 Oct.	Anon.	*New Custome*
13 Oct.	Kyd	*Cornelia*
16 Oct.	Barry	*Ram Alley or Merry Tricks*
26 Oct.	Chapman	*Widow's Tears*
27 Oct.	Tailor	*The Hog Hath Lost His Pearl*
31 Oct.	Heywood	*A Woman Killed with Kindness*
3 Nov. 1878	Fisher [?]	*The True Trojans*
9 Nov.	May	*The Old Couple*
20 Nov.	Peele	*Edward I*
24 Nov.	Peele	*The Old Wive's Tale*
28 Nov.	Peele	*The Arraignment of Paris*
13 Dec.	Davenant	*The Wits*
14 Dec.	Anon.	*The Merry Devil*
18 Dec.	Web. & Row.	*The Thracian Wonder*
22 Dec.	Lodge	*The Wounds of Civil War*
28 Dec.	Tomkis	*Albumazar*
1 Jan. 1879	Habington	*The Queen of Arragon*
6 Jan.	Nash	*Summer's Last Will [and Testament]*
11 Jan.	Suckling	*The Goblins*
19 Jan.	May	*The Heir*
10 Feb.	Brome	*A Jovial Crew*
15 March	Cartwright	*The Ordinary*
6 April	Rowley	*A Match at Midnight*
16 Oct.	Nabbes	*Microcosmus*

20 Oct.	Marlowe	*Lust's Dominion*
20 Oct.	Lyly	*Midas: A Comedy*
10 Nov.	Chapman	*Bussy D'Ambois*
12 Nov.	Rowley	*A New Wonder: A Woman Never Vext*
15 Nov.	Marston	*Parasitaster or The Fawn*
16 Nov.	Lyly	*Endymion*
22 Nov.	Marston	*The Tragedie of Sophonisba*
23 Nov.	Webster	*Appius and Virginia*
24 Nov.	Heywood	*The Golden Age*
28 Nov.	Hey.	*The Silver Age*
30 Nov. 1879	Hey.	*The Brazen Age*
1 Dec.	J.T.	*Grim: The Collier of Croyden*
4 Dec.	Heywood	*First Pt. of The Iron Age*
7 Dec.	Hey.	*Sec. Pt. of The Iron Age*
11 Dec.	Hey.	*The Witches of Lancashire*
1 Jan. 1880	Mayne	*The City-Match*
16 Jan.	Randolph	*The Muse's Looking Glass*
8 Feb.	Heywood	*The English Traveller*
21 Feb.	Chapman	*May Day: A Comedy*
16 March	Heywood	*Royal King and Loyal Subject*
1 April	Chapman	*Monsieur D'Olive*
11 April	Dekker	*The Wonder of a Kingdom*
19 April	Heywood	*A Challenge for Beauty*
25 April	R.B.	*Appius and Virginia*
11 May	Digby	*Elvira*
19 May	Davenport	*The City Night-Cap*
22 May	Killegrew	*The Parson's Wedding*
26 May	Heywood	*The Wise-woman of Hogsdon*
30 May	Hey.	*The Faire Maid of the West*
May	Anon.	*Worlde and the Chylde*
2 Oct.	Heywood	*A Mayden-head Well Lost*
4 Oct.	Shirley	*The Young Admiral*
11 Oct.	Shir.	*The Wedding*
27 Oct.	Heywood	*Faire Maid, Pt. Two*
1 Nov.	Shirley	*The Gamester*
3 Dec.	Shir.	*The Traitor*
December	Shakespeare	**Hamlet*
6 Feb. 1881	Shirley	*The Lady of Pleasure*
15 Feb.	Shir.	*The Example*
Jan. 1882	Jonson	**The Alchemist*
May	Jon.	**The Alchemist*
June	Jon.	**Every Man in His Humour*
July	Jon.	**Poetaster*
July	Jon.	**Volpone*
Aug.	Anon.	*Candlemas Day*
Aug.	Anon.	*Everyman*
Aug.	Anon.	*Hycke-Scorner*
Aug.	Wever	*Lusty Juventus*
Aug.	Jonson	**Sejanus*

Sept.	Preston	*King Cambises*
No Date	BF	*Thierry and Theodoret*
	BF	*Philaster*
	Dekker	*The Kings of Entertainment*
	Ford	*Love's Sacrifice*
	Greene	*James the Fourth*
	Wilkins	*Inforced Marriage*
	Wright	*Historia Histrionica*

Trollope notes in the margin of his copy of Halliwell's *A Dictionary of Old English Plays* that he read the following plays:

13 Jan. 1871	Aphra Behn	*The Rover*
1874 Cokain*	The Obstinate Lady	
1874	Shakespeare	*The Tempest*
	(altered by Davenant** and Dryden)	
11 Ap. 1874	Webster	*The Duchess of Malfey*
Jan. 1875	Dekker	*London's Tempe: Sir James Campbell's Mayoralty*
12 Jan. 1879	Suckling	*Aglaura*
15 Ap. 1882	Congreve***	*The Way of the World*
Aug. 1882	Kyd	*The Spanish Tragedy*
20 Sept. 1882	Anonymous	*The Return from Parnassus*
Sept. 1882	Kyd [?]	*Soliman and Perseda*

* In Halliwell (p. 184) Trollope writes "His works 1874" and it is not clear whether Trollope read the play or owned an 1874 edition of it.

** It is impossible to say, until Trollope's copy is found, how many of Davenant's plays Trollope actually read. In Halliwell Trollope writes "works" beside plays he owned (but may not have read). Beside this edition of the *Tempest* he writes: "Davenants works *read* 1874" (p. 243), but by the other plays of Davenant in the Dictionary, Trollope writes only "works 1673," "works 1873" or "1874". These are the plays by Davenant Trollope has marked in one of these three ways without using the word "read":

The Distresses
The Fair Favourite
Macbeth, Davenant's edition
The Man's the Master
News from Plymouth
A Playhouse to be Let
The Rivals
The Siege of Rhodes

*** In Halliwell, p. 268, Trollope says "His work read — again — April 15 1882"

A LIST OF TROLLOPE'S BOOKS IN THE FOLGER LIBRARY

The asterisk indicates those volumes which have Trollope's manuscript notes.

*Baldwyn, ed. *The Old English Drama: A Selection of Plays from the Old English Dramatists.* 2 vols. London: Hurst, Robinson, and Co., 1825.

*Beaumont, Francis, & Fletcher. *The Works of Beaumont & Fletcher.* Notes by Rev. Alexander Dyce. 11 vols. London: Edward Moxon, 1843-46.

C, I. *A Pleasant Comedy, Called, The Two Merry Milkmaids: or, The Best Words Wear the Garland,* 1661.

*Child, Francis James, ed. *Four Old Plays.* Cambridge: George Nichols, 1848.

*Congreve, William. *Love for Love.* Prompt copy of Charles Macready, 1776. [Trollope's note on when he purchased it]

*Dekker, Thomas. *The Dramatic Works.* 6 vols. London: John Pearson, 1873.

*Dilke, Charles Wentworth, ed. *Old Plays; Being a Continuation of Dodsley's Collection.* 6 vols. London: Rodwell and Martin, 1816.

*Dodsley, Robert, ed. *A Collection of the Old English Plays.* 12 vols. London, 1825-27.

*Ford, John. *The Works of John Ford.* Ed. by William Gifford and Rev. Alexander Dyce. 3 vols. London: James Toovey, 1869.

*Greene, Robert. *The Dramatic Works of Robert Greene.* Ed. by Rev. Alexander Dyce. 2 vols. London: William Pickering, 1831.

*Halliwell-Phillipps, James Orchard. *A Dictionary of Old English Plays.* London: J. R. Smith, 1860. [marginal record of dates]

Hamilton, Anthony, Count. *Memoirs of the English Court, During the Reigns of K. Charles II and K. James II.* London: J. Graves, J. Harbin, et. al., 1719.

*Hawkins, Thomas, ed. *The Origin of the English Drama.* 3 vols. Oxford, 1773. [Folger has only vol. I.]

*Heywood, Thomas. *The Dramatic Works.* 6 vols. London: John Pearson, 1874.

Ingleby, Clement Mansfield. *The Shakespeare Fabrications, or the MS. Notes of the Perkins Folio Shown to be of Recent Origin.* 1859.

Ireland, William Henry. *Vortigern; An Historical Play.* London: J. Thomas, 1832.

*Jonson, Ben. *The Works of Ben Jonson.* 9 vols. London: Bickers and Son, 1875.

*Leveridge, Richard. *A Collection of Songs.* London, 1727. [a page-long note on the flyleaf about Leveridge's life]

*Marlowe, Christopher. *The Works of Christopher Marlowe.* Ed. by Rev. Alexander Dyce. 3 vols. London: William Pickering, 1850.

*Marston, John. *The Works of John Marston.* Ed. by J. O. Halliwell. 3 vols. London: John Russell Smith, 1856.

*Massinger, Philip. *The Plays of Philip Massinger.* Ed. by William Gifford. 4 vols. 1805.

*Middleton, Thomas. *The Works of Thomas Middleton.* Notes by Rev. Alexander Dyce. 5 vols. London: Edward Lumley, 1840.

Oldys, Alexander. *The Fair Extravagant or The Humorous Bride: An English Novel.* London: C. Blount, 1682.

*Otway, Thomas. *The Works of Thomas Otway.* 2 vols. London: J. Tonson, 1712.

*Peele, George. *The Works of George Peele.* Notes by Rev. Alexander Dyce. 2 vols. London: William Pickering, 1828.

Pendragon; or The Carpet Knight His Kalendar. London: J. Newton, 1698.

*Shakespeare, William. *Macbeth.* 1874. [In Icelandic. Trollope's autograph is inside]

*———. *Plays.* With notes by Samuel Johnson and George Steevens. Rev. by Isaac Reed. 6th ed. 21 vols. London: J. Nichols and Son, 1813. [three marginal notes on footnotes; see note on *Macbeth* in Dyce's edition for the longest and most interesting of these notes (Sh,VII,98)]

———. *Teatro Scelto.* 1857-58. [Italian]

———. *Tempest.* London: Macmillan and Co., 1864.

*———. *The Works of Shakespeare.* Rev. by Alexander Dyce. 2nd ed. 9 vols. London: Chapman and Hall, 1866-67.

*Shirley, James. *The Dramatic Works and Poems.* Notes by W. Gifford and Rev. Alexander Dyce. 6 vols. London: J. Murray, 1833.

Waller, Edmund. *The Works of Edmund Waller.* London: J. and R. Tonson and S. Draper, 1744.

*Walmsley, Charles. *A New Theatrical Dictionary.* London: S. Blandon, 1792. [occasional notes on Walmsley's ms. notes]

Ward, Edward. *The London Terraefilius.* London, 1707.